Schools

Look for these and other books in the Lucent
Overview series:

Schools

by Diane Yancey

LUCENT B·O·O·K·S

LUCENT *Overview Series*

Library of Congress Cataloging-in-Publication Data

Yancey, Diane.
    Schools / by Diane Yancey.
        p.   cm. — (Lucent overview series)
    Includes bibliographical references and index.
    ISBN 1-56006-167-7 (alk. paper)
    1. Public schools—United States—Juvenile literature.
    2. Education—United States—Juvenile literature.
    I. Title.   II. Series.
    LA217.2.Y36   1995
    371'.01—dc20
                                              94-40039
                                                  CIP
                                                  AC

Copyright © 1995 by Lucent Books, Inc.
P.O. Box 289011, San Diego, CA 92198-9011
Printed in the U.S.A.

Contents

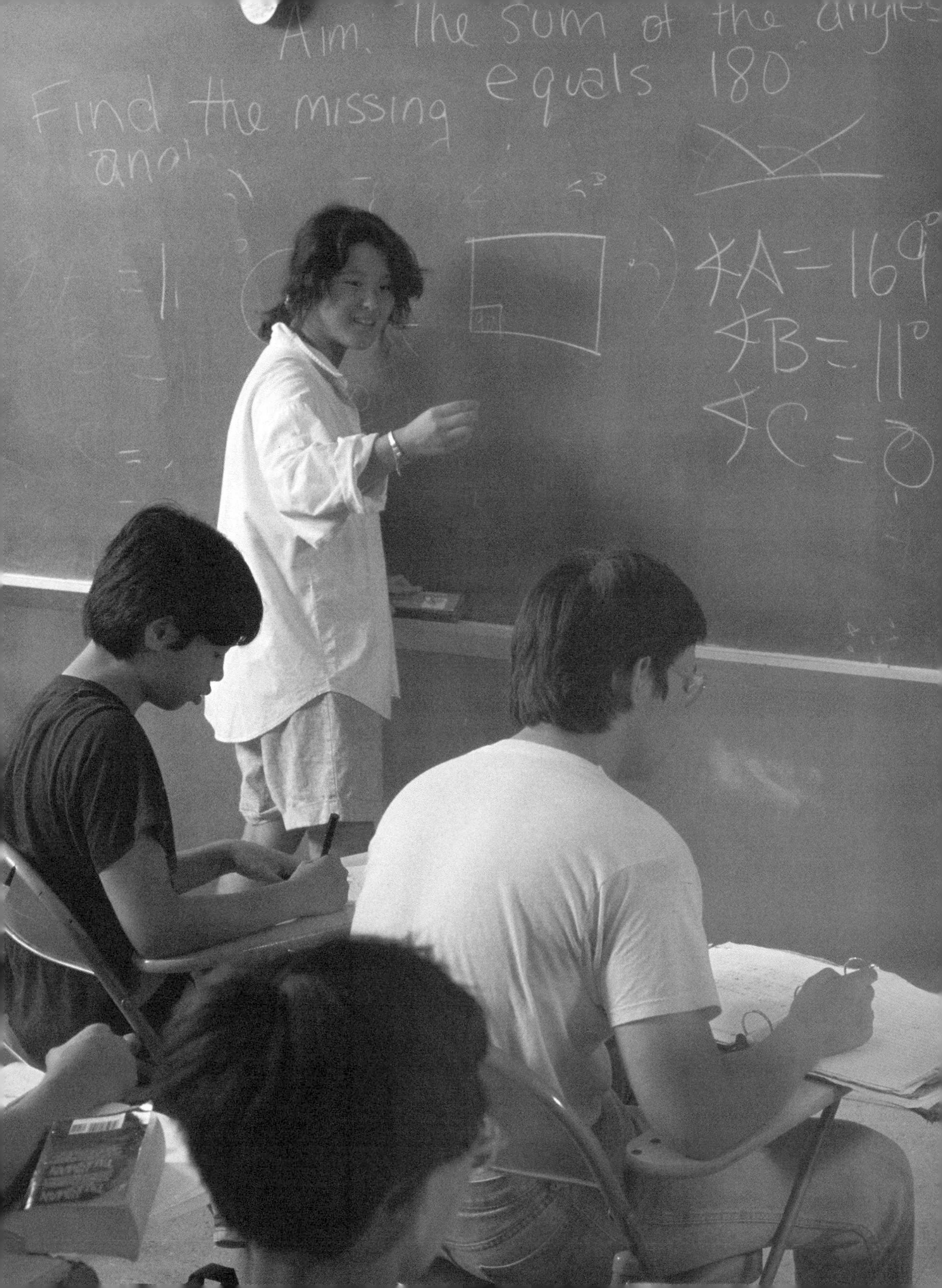
Aim: The sum of the
equals 180°
Find the missing
∡A = 169°
∡B = 11°
∡C = 0

Introduction

FROM THE PRESIDENT OF the United States to the president of the local parent-teacher association (PTA), everyone is talking about schools. More than ever before people recognize the value of a quality education for all Americans. The demand for well-educated, highly skilled workers is growing. Almost one-third of the new jobs created between now and the turn of the century will require a college degree.

Education provides more than skills for careers, however. It teaches self-discipline, creativity, and patience. It prepares people to cope with change. It is invaluable for citizens who must understand and deal with complex social and political issues in a democratic society. As Abraham Lincoln said, "I view [education] as the most important subject which we as a people can be engaged in."

Americans like to think that they share Lincoln's feelings about education. They want to believe that their elementary and secondary schools are doing a good job of teaching. Some evidence can be found to bear out that belief. For instance, in 1989 Sandia National Laboratories, a government research center in Albuquerque, New Mexico, found that Americans' completion rate for

(Opposite page) In a math class, students learn skills that will help them later in life. As the demand for highly skilled workers increases, education becomes invaluable.

7

Many American schools do a fine job of teaching while others struggle to meet this challenge.

high school stood at 85 percent and that nearly 60 percent of young Americans pursued some form of education after graduation from high school. "These rates are the highest in the world," the Sandia report stated. "The overall technical degree attainment by the work force is [also] unparalleled in the world."

At the same time, however, there is evidence that education is suffering from a lack of attention and support. A 1983 report entitled *A Nation at Risk* pointed out that schools were "being eroded by a rising tide of mediocrity" and that Americans had lost sight of the discipline and high expectations needed to obtain a good education. Ten years later a Gallup poll of the public's attitudes toward schools indicated that some, but not enough, improvements had been made. A majority of parents were satisfied with their children's school, yet they gave public schools in general below-average marks, citing concerns about low funding, poor discipline, violence, and drug abuse.

Educators echo those concerns and point to others. "Colleges and universities complain bitterly that professors are now forced to add remedial courses to teach incoming freshmen how to write simple sentences and to compute basic mathematical formulas," education experts Philip Bigler and Karen Lockard write in their 1992 book. Businesspeople, too, are frustrated by secretaries who cannot spell or write a business letter and by machine operators who do not read well enough to understand operating instructions.

Many people wonder why the United States, a country known for its creativity and drive, has not found solutions to the troubles that plague some of the nation's schools. At least part of the answer may lie in the fact that there has been little overall coordination among the nation's approximately ninety thousand elementary and secondary public schools. Unlike schools in other industrialized countries, American schools do not have to meet national standards for what and how they teach. Instead, state and local boards of education set individual policies, standards, and goals. These goals are wide-ranging and often contradictory. Some emphasize the three R's— "reading, 'riting, and 'rithmetic." Others place priority on social education. Some focus on job preparation; others aim to teach students how to think logically and creatively, to evaluate information, and to sort fact from fiction.

Determining nationwide goals

Narrowing these and other priorities into nationwide goals or guidelines has, up to this point, been an unpopular idea with most Americans who support a tradition of community-controlled

As part of his Goals 2000: Educate America Act, President Clinton renewed hope for underprivileged children by expanding the Head Start program.

education. Thus, schools vary from state to state, district to district. Many do a fine job of educating. Others have developed glaring weaknesses that no one has devoted the time or effort to correct.

To emphasize their commitment to better education, two recent presidents have put together plans that they hope will lead the way to improvement. George Bush's America 2000 program included such points as increasing the high school graduation rate to at least 90 percent by the year 2000. Bill Clinton's Goals 2000: Educate America Act, passed by Congress in early 1994, provides funds to aid education through improved curricula—that is, the subjects that a school teaches—instructional materials, and general teaching conditions. The act also supports the development of national education standards.

With all the talk and attention now being given to education, change is on the horizon. Troubled schools must be improved. Good schools must adopt new techniques and new technology in order to meet higher academic expectations. Educators must be flexible and creative as they deal with issues surrounding curriculum, teacher training, funding, school choice, and a host of social problems.

As Secretary of Education Richard W. Riley writes: "We need a drastic overhaul [in education] so that all students have new and better opportunities. . . . Change is difficult, but change we must."

1

How Well Are Schools Doing?

BECAUSE AMERICANS HAVE so many different expectations for education, it is sometimes difficult to determine just how well schools are doing today. Certain undesirable qualities have been defined, but few schools are troubled by all of them, just as few schools are problem free. Most can be said to do an adequate job in some areas and a less than adequate job in others. For instance, a school might have talented teachers but poor administrators, an excellent curriculum but overcrowded facilities.

In spite of the difficulties, there are several common standards by which some people judge schools. The first standard is the success of students—how many graduate, find careers, contribute to the community, and act as responsible citizens. Considering the millions of young people who are successful, a great number of schools must be doing a good job of educating. On the other hand, dropout rates, unemployment, and rising crime seem to show that a significant number of schools fall short of achieving acceptable results.

People also rely on polls, studies, or tests to gauge how well American students are being

(Opposite page) Graduation day symbolizes the hopes and dreams a society has for its young people, and the graduates themselves reflect all that is right and wrong with American schools.

13

At Southern Choctaw High School in Alabama a book props up a broken window. Many decrepit schools have had to forgo repairs because of a lack of funding.

educated. For instance, a survey published by the Center for the Assessment of Educational Progress in 1992 indicated that U.S. students score lower than those in other industrialized nations in such basics as mathematics and science. In its 1992 "Writing Report Card" the Department of Education's National Assessment of Educational Progress revealed that students' writing skills were still poor in spite of slow improvement.

Although comparing test scores is a popular method used to evaluate some types of learning, results are open to interpretation and sometimes cause controversy. One example of this involves falling Scholastic Aptitude Test (SAT) scores, typically a measure of the academic preparedness of American youth. Disturbed by the drop in scores since the 1960s, many people conclude that modern high school students are not as well educated as students have been in the past. Other experts, however, point out that more average students are taking the SAT and planning to go to college today than ever before. Because their test performances are not as high as those of the best students who took the test in the past, average scores are lower.

Despite such controversy, no one denies that there are students in this country who attend inferior schools and get an inferior education. Millions of educators and parents would like to see those schools improved. To do that they study schools that bring out the best in their students as well as those that do not. In time they hope to make fine schools the norm for children everywhere.

Successful schools

Schools that successfully educate students come in a variety of sizes and styles. All have flaws, but they somehow manage to rise above them. Some cater only to the most motivated children; others attempt to educate all who come through their doors. Some have plenty of money, well-equipped facilities, and the best teachers. Others make do with less and still provide an excellent education.

One example of a successful school is Thayer Junior/Senior High School in the small town of Winchester, New Hampshire. Thayer is different from most public schools in that schedules are relaxed—no bells ring at the end of each hour—and classes are informal. Sofas, rocking chairs, and tables replace traditional desks. Teachers help students to think creatively, to be independent, and to care for others. Projects are practical and varied, and students must demonstrate certain learning skills and general academic knowledge before they can graduate. Life After Thayer classes are mandatory to give seniors information about careers, advice on handling social issues, and lessons in skills such as apartment hunting and budgeting.

As a result of time spent in this disciplined yet supportive atmosphere, nearly 95 percent of Thayer students graduate and over half of those get some type of higher education. One teacher explains the school's success in the book *Schools That Work* by saying, "Kids leave with a better sense of who they are, how they fit into society as a whole . . . ; they leave here with a strong sense of . . . what their options are, what they can be."

Located several hundred miles south of Thayer Junior/Senior High is another example of a successful public school, Malcolm X Elementary. Malcolm X is located in one of the toughest neighborhoods in Washington, D.C., and seems to succeed against all odds. Outside its boundaries sirens and gunfire are common. Inside the staff combines encouragement, high expectations, and firm discipline to provide inspiration and a safe environment for students. Everyone, from the principal to the security guard, works together to convince high-risk children that education is their ticket to a better life. Students' test scores are not as high as those of well-to-do suburban children, but attendance at Malcolm X runs at 93 percent.

Fifth graders are hard at work at Malcolm X Elementary School in Washington, D.C. A combination of encouragement, high expectations, and firm discipline has helped the school succeed against all odds.

Increasing numbers of parents volunteer their time at the school and make sure their children attend class and complete homework. Students who might otherwise drop out are motivated to learn.

"I can honestly say my daughter will have a great future," parent Tyrone Woods states in the December 1992 issue of *Time*. Debra Tracy, another parent, adds, "This is a school you can be proud to send your child to."

Troubled schools

Americans often picture inadequate schools as small country facilities, isolated from the latest trends and technology. This picture is only partially accurate. Children of migrant workers, sharecroppers, and the rural poor are often poorly educated because of inferior schools, unsettled lifestyles, and too little emphasis on learning. However, the majority of schools that fail to adequately educate large numbers of students lie within the heart of inner cities across the nation.

In his book *Savage Inequalities*, author and educator Jonathan Kozol focuses on many such schools. Some of the most troubled are located in East St. Louis, Illinois, where children study in dilapidated buildings with broken windows and dark halls. There are no playgrounds. Science laboratory equipment is over thirty years old. Libraries are understocked. Teacher layoffs are frequent, and the dropout rate is high. Says one high school teacher:

> I have four girls right now in my senior homeroom who are pregnant or have just had babies. When I ask them why this happens, I am told, "Well, there's no reason not to have a baby. There's not much for me in public school."

Other examples of troubled schools can be found in Chicago's inner city. Over half of the

Peeling paint and large holes in the ceiling of this New York high school clearly illustrate the need for additional funding.

high schools there turn out students who score, on the average, in the bottom 1 percent on national college-entrance examinations. School buildings are run-down. Gang violence and drug abuse are common occurrences.

Pamela Price, a concerned Chicagoan, described her first visit to one school: "Kids were running everywhere. Teachers were sneaking out the back door going to the store. Kids were coming to school at 10 and 11 o'clock."

Funding and schools

There are many schools like Thayer and Malcolm X across the country, just as there are hundreds like those in East St. Louis and Chicago that badly need improvement. Each one, good or bad, has the potential to provide a first-class education. That potential is affected by a combination of factors that include funding, management, teachers, parents, and community involvement. When these factors combine in a good mix, schools can be almost certain of success. When these factors go wrong, however, doing a good job of educating students becomes an almost impossible task.

The first factor that affects education is funding. Although money does not guarantee a school's success, it is vital for maintaining buildings, purchasing books and supplies, and offering enrichment programs that can spark enthusiasm for learning.

When adequate funds are unavailable, school programs and purchases dry up. Fewer teachers are hired, and those who are hired are generally inexperienced, so they can be paid lower salaries. Textbooks are not replaced. Laboratories are shut down for lack of supplies.

Underfunding also leads to overcrowding, another serious threat to good teaching. In crowded schools class size may reach more than forty students. Desks are packed together. Halls and cafeterias are jammed. Discipline problems are more likely simply because there is little room for anyone to move freely.

In Southern California overcrowding has reached crisis proportions in the last decade because of tight budgets and a constant stream of immigrant students who swell enrollments. In 1992 California state superintendent of schools Bill Honig said that his state would need to build a new six-hundred-student school every day for five years just for existing schools to maintain their already overcrowded conditions. Adequate construction is not taking place, and the student population continues to grow.

Management

Management is another factor that can affect the success of schools. Although school districts need good administrators who understand the needs of the students and families they serve, experience has shown that schools function best when given the freedom to manage themselves. As Joseph Fernandez, former chancellor, or head,

A Los Angeles Unified School District administrator motions to one of hundreds of schools awaiting much needed repairs.

of New York City's one thousand public schools, points out:

> A school system, like everything else, works better if people talk to one another, if people plan together, if people apply what they know at the source of a problem *to* the problem.

With a policy known as site-based management (SBM), all that takes place. In almost 60 percent of schools across the country, local management teams or councils—usually made up of parents, teachers, students, and community members—meet regularly and make a range of decisions about financing, hiring and firing of staff, approving educational goals, and developing curricula. The SBM policy provides increased flexibility in the way schools operate, involves parents

Students in Queens, New York, overflow into lunchrooms as classrooms have become too crowded. Many advocates of site-based management hope that this policy will help curb overcrowding and other problems in public schools.

in decision making, and improves student attendance because of personalized attention.

Although site-based management is generally viewed as a good thing, it has its negative aspects. "Empowering parents is risky business," says Willie W. Herenton, superintendent of schools in Memphis, Tennessee, where site-based management was introduced in seven schools in late 1989. "You get all the dynamics of human interaction. Some parents want to control. Some don't understand much about how schools function. It's a give and take arrangement."

Chicago, home to one of the first SBM experiments, can testify that SBM has reduced, but not eliminated, the ills found in many of its six hundred schools. Five years after independent school councils were given authority by the Illinois legislature to try to improve the city's troubled schools, conditions are still discouraging. Discipline has tightened, but the district's $300 million budget deficit may cause teacher layoffs. Students have new textbooks, but test scores remain low, and the high school dropout rate has increased. The councils, given only limited authority, claim that bureaucracy is hampering their efforts.

Problems with bureaucracy

Bureaucracy—layers of administration operating under inflexible rules and regulations—is an enemy of good management in almost all large school districts. Over time dozens of administrative offices and programs have been formed to deal with issues such as security, dropout prevention, and testing. While most programs are useful and necessary, carelessness, waste, and dishonesty are common. Change is difficult. Time and money needed to maintain the complicated system continually drain resources away from the primary goal, the education of students.

An after-school program that provides students with extra help requires the dedication of teachers and students alike.

After coping with bureaucracy for long periods of time, caring teachers, parents, and students become frustrated and apathetic, or indifferent. Parents in Chicago speak bitterly of their continuing powerlessness. "The politicians, the board—they don't listen to us," says Shekiya Yehuda, a Chicago school council member. "These people do what they want to do. . . . We don't have any power. We never did."

Teachers

Teachers also make a difference in how well a school educates, or fails to educate, its students. Poor teachers are boring, unprepared, or unable to maintain discipline in even the best of classes. On the other hand, good teachers do best when they have freedom to express themselves, to improvise, and to manage discipline.

The trademark of a good teacher is often an unconventional approach to teaching. For example, one Louisiana teacher, Debbie Pace Silver, illustrates the concept of inertia (the tendency of a moving body to remain in motion) by gliding around the classroom on roller skates. Another—James Ellingson of Moorehead, Minnesota—sends his science students out to the school yard to collect "worms," colored toothpicks he has sprinkled over the lawn. The experience gives students the opportunity to understand protective coloration and practice collecting and recording scientific data.

Parents

Not only good teachers but also good parents help schools succeed. When parents are interested and involved in education, they communicate that interest to their children. When parents volunteer to chaperone dances, grade papers, and carry out other routine activities, they not only show their commitment to schools, they give teachers time to concentrate on students rather than paperwork. As writer and education expert Anne Henderson explains in *America's Best Classrooms:*

> Children whose parents help them at home and stay in touch with the school score higher than children . . . whose parents are not involved. Schools where children are failing improve dramatically when parents are called in to help.

Children from fragmented families or families that do not recognize the benefits of education are at an increased risk of failure in schools today. Many face the extra handicap of extreme poverty and come to school hungry. In some inner cities, where a large proportion of children fall into these categories, producing well-educated students is a difficult proposition.

Children in these circumstances receive little encouragement to do well in school. Often there is no one at home after school to praise them for doing well or to listen to their problems. Afternoons are passed on the street with friends. At night television takes the place of homework.

Children living in dysfunctional families, or families that function abnormally, face even greater obstacles. In these homes, addicted,

Teacher Roger Socci and his third grade students show off their "Magic Mall." This scaled-down version of a modern shopping mall allows students to "shop" for facts.

Offering support and guidance, an involved father helps his daughter with her homework.

troubled, or abusive parents are often too self-involved to see that their children get an education. In many cases children come to school too angry, fearful, or exhausted to study.

Students who lack family support are often not prepared to enter school. They have not been taught self-discipline or respect for teachers and school rules. Thus, they fail to follow directions, to concentrate on lessons, or to get along with others. Not understanding the long-term benefits of a good education, they may prefer the quick payback of an unskilled job—or perhaps even turn to crime—and drop out of school in spite of the efforts of educators to persuade them otherwise.

Communities

Involvement by businesses and other community organizations can negate some of the damage to children caused by a lack of family support. When businesspeople or other volunteers coach after-school sports or sponsor field trips, they act as positive role models. Financial support from the community and other organizations can provide programs and services that are not included in school budgets. For example, in 1992 contributions from Footlocker, Illinois Bell, and Nike supported Chicago schools' athletic programs, which would otherwise have been cut for lack of funds.

"Schools that relate well to their communities have student bodies that outperform other schools," points out Anne Henderson.

Without strong support from the community, schools can become settings for violence and crime. Students without goals or adult role models are more likely to give in to peer pressure. Children from broken or abusive homes, or those who are frequently left on their own, often join

gangs that take the place of families and exert a negative influence on behavior.

Although problems with drugs, guns, and gangs are not new challenges for America, they cause an increasing number of problems in schools today. According to a 1994 report 270,000 guns are carried into school every week. Students as young as fourth or fifth graders are arming themselves, either to be like older kids or to protect themselves.

"If you had the money, you could get yourself a 'tool' in fifteen minutes," one New York City sophomore says in the March 1992 issue of *Newsweek.* "I would say, out of 100 kids, 90 got guns or can get them."

The problem is not limited to inner-city schools either. In small towns and middle-class communities across the nation, violence is disrupting education. One example is an episode that

Without proper role models or supportive families, many students turn to gangs. These teenagers belong to a gang in Los Angeles.

took place in March 1994 in Ballard, a quiet suburb of Seattle, Washington. While waiting for a ride home from school, sixteen-year-old Melissa Fernandes was fatally wounded when a carload of gang-affiliated teens drove past and fired off a random shot. Melissa died the next day. Fernandes's mother had moved her daughter to Ballard High School to avoid the violence reported in her previous school.

Educators alone can do little to stem this violence, which usually begins on the streets and spills over to school grounds. Some districts are implementing strict dress codes or even requiring school uniforms. They hope this move will reduce peer pressure to wear expensive brand-name clothes and shoes that are often gang related. Other schools have resorted to removing lockers—a logical place to hide drugs and weapons—hiring security guards, and installing metal detectors. Over one-quarter of the nation's large city schools now use detectors to screen students for weapons before they enter school buildings.

Mount View High School in West Virginia installed metal detectors at the school's entrance after a student brought a gun to school and shot another student.

Students watch as a shooting victim is carried out of Woodrow Wilson High School in Washington. Scenes such as this have been witnessed across the country.

"The school setting is almost impossible to police without tyrannical dictatorship," says Mark Karlin of the Illinois Council Against Handgun Violence. "[Schools] are in an impossible situation . . . we expect them to do what the rest of us cannot."

Working for improvement

America is blessed with some of the best schools in the world. It is also burdened with some that badly need help. Improvement is possible, but careful planning will be vital. Poorly thought-out, poorly managed programs may only make problems worse. This is especially true with regard to curricula. What schools teach and how they teach has become one of the most hotly debated issues in education circles today.

2

More than the
Three R's

CHOOSING CURRICULUM—the subjects that a school teaches—seems as though it ought to be a relatively easy task. After all, everybody needs to be taught how to read, write, add, and subtract. All a teacher has to do is add a little science, social studies, and art, and the education menu is complete.

In reality, however, creating specific programs that satisfy everyone proves more difficult. For instance, some Americans, such as Ernest Boyer of the Carnegie Foundation for the Advancement of Teaching, believe that curricula should be based on "a core of common learning . . . a study of those . . . ideas, experiences, and traditions common to all of us."

Others believe that "a core of common learning" is not necessary or desirable. Because of the diversity in America, traditions and values may be one thing to a rancher's son in Montana and something entirely different to a lawyer's daughter in Florida. Thus, students need to be exposed to differences that challenge them to think in new ways.

Curriculum discussions extend to other equally important issues, including which subjects

(Opposite page) Education for third graders at Wingdale Elementary School in New York goes beyond the three R's. Curriculum includes computer classes.

deserve the most time and attention, how those subjects should be presented, and whether certain subjects have any place at all in public education. As schools reform their curricula and stretch to cover an increasing number of subjects—some of them controversial—many Americans are demanding that priorities be set. They ask if some topics might better be handled outside the school setting.

What is being taught?

Although people have many different opinions about what schools ought to teach, participants in the debate can be loosely divided into two groups: those who prefer a traditional curriculum and those who do not.

Traditionalists see a good curriculum as one that concentrates on knowledge and skills, such as multiplication tables, rules of grammar, and dates and events in history. Traditionalists believe education should be an organized process, with results measured by test scores. In order to achieve those results, traditionalists believe in longer school days, regular homework, plenty of

Traditionalists stress the need for a curriculum focused on testing, homework, and discipline. They believe this sort of education provides students with the knowledge and skills necessary for future success.

discipline from teachers and parents, and a narrowing of curriculum. For example, they would eliminate classes such as calligraphy or video production.

People who support nontraditional curricula feel that the purpose of schools is to teach more than facts and figures. A curriculum should help students learn to think. It should help them learn more about themselves and humankind, such as why people behave the way they do, why certain events have taken place, and how we can learn from history. Nontraditionalists are not against academics, but they point out that in a fast-changing world people cannot learn all the facts they will need to know in their lifetime. If, however, students are taught to become creative thinkers and problem solvers, they are then likely to develop into adults who love learning and who will contribute to the improvement of their world.

A Chicago math teacher helps a student learn geometric shapes by completing puzzles. Exercises such as this also teach students creative thinking and problem-solving skills.

Varied Curriculum

In school today curriculum seems to be a veritable tossed salad of traditional and nontraditional subjects. As education commentator Anthony Giardina writes, "The schools have, in effect, been asked to do everything, to educate the mind, to educate the body, to build self-esteem, to offer ways to solve conflicts."

Former New York schools chancellor Joseph Fernandez comments:

> With traditional core studies squeezed from all sides, school curricula now run the gamut [range] from safe driving to safe sex. Teachers unravel the mysteries of everything from "race relations" and "conflict resolution" to table manners.

In elementary schools, where curricula almost always include reading, spelling, arithmetic, and social studies, an abundance of other subjects is taught according to legislative mandate, or orders,

Posted outside a Virginia elementary school, this sign reinforces the school's drug awareness program. Growing concern over drug use has caused many schools to start similar programs.

district requirements, and teachers' personal interests. Many states require a host of safety programs such as earthquake preparedness, gun safety, and drug awareness. Physical education and music classes are usually squeezed into the weekly schedule, along with a monthly visit from the school counselor or a volunteer art instructor. Teachers might use spare time for science projects or for taking on community-service projects such as roadside cleanup or recycling.

In high school the options broaden. Requirements still include mathematics and English, but choices for those courses range from remedial mathematics to calculus, from basic English to creative writing and drama. Most schools offer vocational technology courses, college preparatory courses, and driver education and business courses, as well as a variety of other electives ranging from photography to work experience, cheerleading to T-shirt design.

Because states and districts vary in their methods of determining what a complete and well-balanced curriculum should be, the question arises whether students are getting the right balance of subjects—science versus the arts, academic subjects such as mathematics versus social topics such as AIDS education. Parents ask if students learn enough mathematics to get good jobs and to be competitive with students from other countries. Educators look at the variety of standards set by school districts and wonder if a high school diploma earned in a Tennessee school, for instance, is equivalent to a high school diploma earned in Idaho or California or New York.

The answers are not clear because school quality varies so widely. Evidence shows, however, that even in schools with high standards, many students just get by rather than acquire a first-class education. In too many schools students are able to satisfy graduation requirements with classes such as general science or basic mathematics, rather than more difficult ones such as chemistry or calculus. They are allowed to pass courses with C's or D's rather than thoroughly learning class material and earning A's or B's.

Enough time to learn

As people focus on what schools are teaching, they also ask if enough time is being allowed for students to thoroughly learn the subjects to which they are exposed. Because of the increased number of required subjects, mathematics time must be shortened to allow time for drug prevention programs. English makes way for stress management or conflict resolution. Taken together, cutbacks to basic subjects are sometimes dramatic, as Joseph Fernandez relates in his book *Tales Out of School:*

> A friend of mine was talking with a second-grade teacher at an urban school in the East. My friend asked her how much math, spelling, reading, and science she thought she was giving her students. "About five hours," she said.
>
> "That's not so bad," my friend observed. "Five hours a day should be more than enough."
>
> "No, not five hours a day," replied the teacher. "Five hours a week."

Traditionalists point out that sufficient time for learning would be available if curricula were narrowed and all but the basics eliminated. Others suggest that a better answer might lie in lengthening the school year. Although many districts have found that staggered-schedule, year-round schooling is beneficial to improve learning, relieve overcrowding, and keep kids off the streets, most students still go to school only an average of 180 days a year. Supporters of a longer school year point out that German students attend about 210 days a year; Japanese, around 240.

The experiment with a longer school year is already at work in a few places across the country. Two elementary schools in New Orleans, Louisiana, began the experiment in 1989, when the school year there was lengthened to 220 days. "Come September, I'm ready to get into the meat of reading. Normally, I can't do that until the end of October," says a second-grade teacher, Juanita Smith. Smith appreciates the fact that students on a shortened summer vacation do not have time to forget what they learned the year before.

Going to school for additional days, however, means higher costs to keep school buildings

At Harding Elementary School in Michigan, a class practices multiplication. Time allotted for basic subjects such as math is often shortened as new subjects are added to school curricula.

open, to run buses, and to pay teachers. In 1991 California estimated that lengthening the school year across the state would cost $121 million a day. That increased cost makes the change out of the question for the many school districts already operating on tight budgets.

An informal approach

Along with the question of what should be taught come concerns with methodology, or how subjects should be presented. In many schools teachers are turning away from the use of textbooks, which students find boring, in favor of class discussion and supplementary material such as that found in newsmagazines, on computer software programs, and on cable television. For instance, at Hubbard Woods Elementary School in Winnetka, Illinois, second-grade students learn about pioneers by reading books such as those by fiction writer Laura Ingalls Wilder and through writing assignments and discussions about settlers on the frontier. Spelling lessons and artwork also relate to this theme.

Teachers insist that as a result of this approach education is seen as enjoyable and important rather than something to avoid. Student attitudes support this argument as well. "We don't need those books over there," says one Hubbard Woods second grader, pointing to a shelf of textbooks. "We have real books to read."

Despite its popularity, some parents and educators are troubled by the informality of this method. They admit that textbooks can be uninteresting but point out that texts present information in a more complete and systematic way than discussions or novels and other supplementary material. They worry that students may not think about such basics as rules of punctuation or grammar when they sit down to watch a video or read a newspaper.

In Marin County, California, a teacher watches as her student works on the computer. Some teachers have turned away from traditional textbooks as their primary teaching tools.

In another effort to improve learning, many schools across the country are adopting a strategy of teaching known as outcome-based education (OBE), sometimes called performance-based education. Under this system, students are expected to demonstrate in a practical way that they understand and can use certain information and skills that are taught in school. Learning may include social values such as cooperation and communication, as well as more traditional academic subjects.

OBE can be compared to the system by which Boy Scouts earn merit badges. It is different from traditional learning approaches in that students are allowed to progress at their own pace, mastering one skill before moving on to the next. OBE assumes that all students are able to learn, given enough time and the right materials. Teachers do less lecturing to the class as a whole and spend more time with one-on-one guidance. Goals and specific details of curricula are set by states or school districts. Students must demonstrate a command of required subjects and skills before they can graduate from high school.

Objections to OBE

Although OBE promises to do away with the problem of high school graduates who cannot read, write, or do mathematics, the new strategy has its critics. Many object to OBE plans that heavily promote values that parents do not believe in. Other people worry that OBE may eventually prove to be an ineffective method of learning. They fear that too much emphasis will be placed on gaining skills such as creative thinking and that, in the process, academic subjects will be neglected.

Perhaps the greatest concern about OBE, however, is that the new technique will not demand enough from students, that students will no longer be challenged to learn as much or as well. Critics remark that if every child playing basketball was required to make a basket, wouldn't the hoop have to be lowered to achieve that goal. On the other hand, if standards are not lowered, people wonder if some children will have to remain in school for years after they would normally graduate in order to master required facts and skills.

Multicultural education

Another approach to learning that causes debate is multiculturalism—the movement to include more information about different cultures, languages, and customs in school curricula. For centuries history and literature textbooks were written from the Eurocentric perspective; that is, interpreting the world from a Western perspective. Additionally, the exploits of white males such as Christopher Columbus and George Washington were emphasized. The feelings, beliefs, and con-

Many educators feel that school curricula should include a variety of cultural, historical, and political perspectives.

tributions of other groups were poorly represented.

Today, as the percentage of non-European races increases rapidly in the United States, that approach is changing. In schools in some states—California, New Mexico, and Texas, for instance—population estimates show that almost half of all classes will be made up of nonwhite students by 1995. Many feel that a Eurocentric education is no longer appropriate for Americans. New York State education commissioner Thomas Sobol wrote in 1990:

> We cannot understand American history, nor many of the social and political phenomena [events] of the present, without also understanding the African American experience . . . and the same is true of the Native American experience and the experience of Latino and Asian peoples, as well as all of the varied groups who have helped to shape our institutions and our sensibilities.

Many states have already acted on this belief. In 1987 California schools introduced a multicultural social studies curriculum. New York City schools came out in 1992 with their Children of the Rainbow curriculum that promotes tolerance toward different people and lifestyles.

Although the goal of multicultural curricula is

to teach awareness and understanding, many Americans worry that it may hurt more than it helps. They fear that some educators, while emphasizing the experiences and contributions of a variety of races and cultures, may subtly revise history by teaching it inaccurately. For instance, if multiculturalists teach that many cultures have contributed to the makeup of the United States, they may not make clear to students that American society—its language, system of government, and ideas about individual liberty—was, for the most part, modeled on European examples.

Others worry that instead of encouraging tolerance and appreciation for differences, multicultural education will fan the fires of racism and discourage national unity. With a multicultural approach, ethnic groups are urged to take pride in remembering and maintaining their cultural roots.

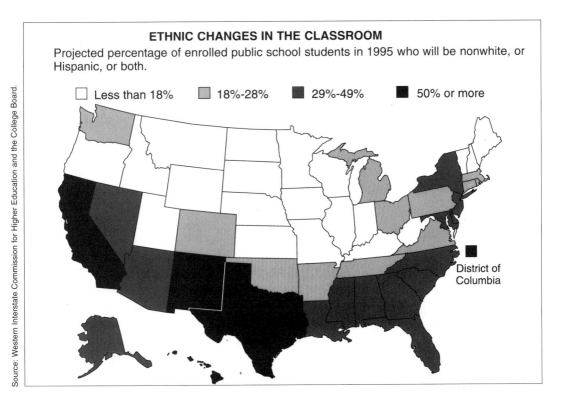

ETHNIC CHANGES IN THE CLASSROOM

Projected percentage of enrolled public school students in 1995 who will be nonwhite, or Hispanic, or both.

☐ Less than 18%　　▨ 18%-28%　　▨ 29%-49%　　■ 50% or more

District of Columbia

Source: Western Interstate Commission for Higher Education and the College Board.

They are encouraged to value their differences as much as or more than American traditions and institutions. "It is surely not the office [duty] of the public school to promote ethnic separatism and heighten ethnic tensions," says historian and Pulitzer Prize winner Arthur Schlesinger Jr.

Values education

With a growing emphasis on teaching tolerance, the issue of values education has also arisen in schools today. Public schools are caught between people who object to the teaching of values with which they disagree, and people who protest the absence of values education in the curriculum.

In general, values can be defined as the moral and ethical standards that guide a person in determining right from wrong. Honesty, loyalty, perseverance, and respect are all admired standards of behavior in this society. For example, most Americans agree that cheating on a test is wrong and that standing by a troubled friend is admirable.

Values such as these are usually passed from parents to children, but values have always been taught in schools, too, although not necessarily as part of the curriculum. Teachers encourage fairness in class and on the playground. They discourage cheating and disruptive behavior. Few people object to this type of lesson in school or in any other setting.

Objections arise, however, when classroom discussions turn to subjects on which people have strong differences of opinion. Not everyone agrees on what is right and what is wrong. With some subjects, nearly any approach will thrust a teacher or school into the middle of a values debate.

Teen sexuality is one such subject. Health and sex education are part of school curricula in many districts, but there is often disagreement about course content. Some parents argue that sex

education does not belong in school at all. Others say discussion should be limited. For example, high school health courses should stress the importance of abstinence until marriage and omit discussion of other options. Still other people argue that young people must have complete, age-appropriate information in order to make responsible decisions about their own behavior.

The subject of birth control can be even more controversial. A teacher who includes discussions of birth control may be accused of condoning sex between teenagers. A teacher who omits discussion of birth control may be criticized for presenting an incomplete picture of the subject matter. Parents on both sides can, and do, argue that the schools' approach violates their personal moral values.

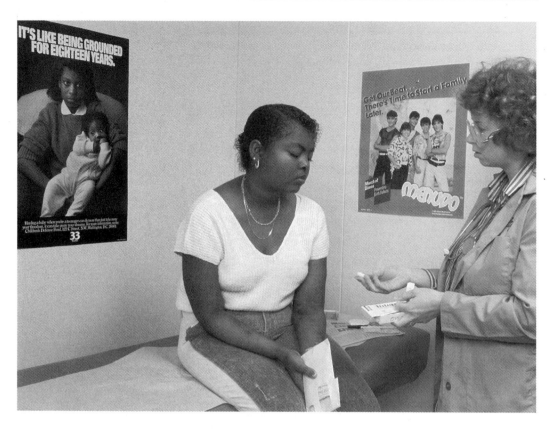

Birth control is discussed and dispensed in a Dallas school clinic.

Although most people prefer that values be taught in the family, too many parents fail to teach standards to their children. "[The idea of] raising moral questions is, to some, troubling, disquieting, and threatening," says David E. Purpel, professor of education at the University of North Carolina. Rather than let generations of young people grow up without a knowledge of right and wrong, many Americans believe that schools should take the responsibility for instilling values.

In the words of John Martin Rich, professor in the Department of Education at the University of Austin, Texas, "[Schools must] strive to be centers of inquiry where moral conflicts are examined, a place where youth can learn to make intelligent moral judgments."

As some school districts are learning, disagreements over curriculum can turn into battles that can disrupt learning. Hundreds of parents have turned out to protest the use of the Impressions reading series, a curriculum published in 1984 that includes short stories, poems, and novel excerpts, many of which have frightening and violent themes. In 1991 one California school district was taken to court over Impressions, spending money and energy that could otherwise have been used for student-related projects.

A similar dispute made news in New York City in 1993, when several school boards and parents objected to material on homosexual families being included in the city's Children of the Rainbow curriculum. Opposition helped lead to heated school board elections, the resignation of Chancellor Joseph Fernandez, and a lengthy analysis of the material.

It is not just curriculum that makes people angry, however. Surprisingly, extracurricular programs stir up controversy as well. These extras may be optional, but their presence or absence can cause as much dispute as more weighty educational issues that arise today.

A sex education teacher asks her students to write about their concept of love.

3

A Look at the Extras

WHEN WESTSIDE HIGH SCHOOL in Omaha, Nebraska, refused to let student Bridget Mergens set up an after-school religious club on campus in 1990, Bridget took her case to court. She won, but her opponents continue to argue that the presence of such clubs at school is a violation of the separation of church and state and, therefore, unconstitutional.

In New York City in 1991 politicians, parents, and clergy rallied to protest the board of education's decision to make condoms available in the city's high schools. Some people resented the board's endorsing a policy that seemed to weaken parental supervision and authority. Others believed the financially strapped school system could have found better ways to spend public money.

Clearly, extracurricular programs are no longer limited to such traditional activities as football, baseball, and honor society. Instead, students express themselves through options that range from soccer to scuba diving, art to environmental cleanup. Schools provide health services to help with physical and emotional needs. Social welfare programs that include low-cost meals, after-school day care, and babysitting for teenage

(Opposite page) In addition to the traditional extracurricular programs offered by schools, some schools also provide health and social welfare programs. These students are participating in a discussion of abortion.

45

mothers have been set up to help at-risk students as well.

Extracurricular activities are also used to make academic subjects more interesting. Says Theresa Noonan, a teacher at Gulf Breeze High School in Florida:

> We are always fighting for the extracurricular programs that make the classroom come alive. . . . Whether it's a trip to Washington to study the government or a trip to the Florida Keys to study marine biology, . . . we see the need to make the classroom come alive and be more relevant to these kids' lives.

Health clinics and teen counseling

In recent years Americans have become aware that large numbers of students regularly cope with problems that range from stress to emotional and physical abuse, from drug and alcohol addiction to eating disorders and pregnancy. Often parents lack the knowledge, the will, or the funds to get help for their children. Children can be too embarrassed or too frightened to turn to parents or a family doctor with their questions or concerns. Yet for students who experience any of these problems, learning can be difficult, if not impossible.

School health clinics and counseling centers can provide students with help in dealing with delicate personal and family problems.

In an effort to make health services more accessible to students, on-campus clinics and counselors have become an integral part of school services in recent decades. In some cases healthcare staff simply advise, hand out brochures, and direct students to further resources. At other times the staff is able to do more. For instance, on-campus family resource centers in Kentucky provide immunization services to children who are just starting school. School-based clinics in Texas provide checkups for pregnant teens, enabling them to get more frequent care than they might if they had to seek out off-campus clinics.

Although school nurses and counselors, trained to recognize and advise troubled students, can make a positive difference, they are sometimes unappreciated. Many parents are embarrassed by their children's talking to strangers about personal feelings or family problems. "When kids come to me, they're telling me family secrets," says Leslie Giordano, a Massachusetts school psychologist. "I'm not prying things out of them. . . . They tell me things because they're in pain. So I'm a threat [to parents]."

Parental protest

Other parents object to young people's having easy access to information about birth control, abortion, and homosexuality. Condom distribution—a school response to the growing numbers of teens who are infected with AIDS or who are HIV positive—is one of the most unpopular and hotly debated topics. Certain parents and educators believe the program encourages teen promiscuity. They would rather schools urge abstinence than provide condoms. "If they're not going to teach that sex before marriage is wrong, they shouldn't be teaching anything at all," says Melinda Di Mambro, an Oklahoma mother of four.

More than sixty school districts across the nation have made condoms available to students through school clinics. Parental protests have defeated programs in other districts. Those programs that remain carry on their work with the support of those who believe that all measures must be taken to help teens protect themselves. States Jeanne Kiefner, a New Jersey school nurse:

> I'm aware of the . . . ideological battlegrounds, political impact, and financial problems involved in a public school condom distribution program, but . . . we've got a professional responsibility to provide adolescents with the necessary information to help them make intelligent health choices.

Value of extras

Americans debate not only the value of health clinics and counseling services in schools; some believe that there may be other extracurricular programs whose elimination could benefit students and teachers alike. For instance, with fewer football or basketball practices, students would have extra hours to study every afternoon. Cutbacks of out-of-town games, music and drama rehearsals, and other activities that take students out of classes could also help improve academic performance.

Educators, too, might appreciate fewer after-school programs. "I spend all Wednesday afternoon at games and all day Saturday at games," one Massachusetts teacher muses in Susan Moore Johnson's book *Teachers at Work*. "It's exhausting. Perhaps if that time weren't consumed by coaching, I could spend more time thinking up new ideas."

While most people agree that extracurricular programs should not interfere with academics, some point out that some activities provide enrichment that academic programs cannot. Organi-

zations such as the Future Educators of America encourage and inform young people who are interested in exploring careers in education. Chess clubs and computer clubs supplement mathematics, science, and technology courses. And as Joseph Fernandez points out in *Tales Out of School*, most educators recognize "the positive attention and unifying spirit a good athletic program can bring to a school."

Certain extracurricular programs do more than entertain and encourage. They can be tools to improve the academic performances of students. A music project entitled Blues in School is a case in point. This after-school program was founded in 1990 in Charleston, South Carolina, by local businessperson Mary Edelman, who believes that young people involved with music are less apt to get into trouble. "When you . . . give them an opportunity, it creates hope, and with hope . . . there are no limits to what they can accomplish," she says.

Children from several inner-city middle

Allowing students to participate in extracurricular activities can build self-esteem and give even the failing student a sense of purpose.

schools in the area are taught that the blues are "our history, our culture, and the roots of American music" and are also given a chance to sing and perform in the community and at competitions. The program helps students make new friends and gives them a sense of purpose that builds self-esteem. That sense of purpose often translates into better learning.

"I always used to get into a lot of trouble in school," says Lawrence Brown, one of the participants in the program. "I was flunking everything except for two subjects. After I got in 'Blues in School,' I ended up passing everything."

Community service

Another extracurricular activity, community service, is also recognized for its benefit to students. Although service clubs such as Key Club have existed on many high school campuses for years, educators are now placing new emphasis on community involvement because of the boost it can give to students' self-esteem and interest in learning.

For instance, at Thomas Jefferson High School in South Central Los Angeles, students who are involved in the school's community-service program have a 96 percent attendance rate compared to overall school attendance, which runs at only 75 percent. At least 98 percent of community-service participants at Thomas Jefferson go on to college. Says project leader and social studies teacher Chris Gutierrez:

> Last spring we asked our tenth graders to tell us how they envisioned themselves 10 years from now. . . . They mentioned wanting to take care of their families, wanting to give to their communities. And many said they hoped to be teachers.

Because community service is seen as having a positive effect on students, encouraging them to develop qualities of kindness and unselfishness and to be more responsible citizens, policy makers have begun to stress its importance as well. In November 1990 President George Bush signed into law the National and Community Service Act, which provided funds to set up community-service programs in schools and colleges across the nation.

In 1992 Maryland became the first state to make community service mandatory in high school. The board of education in that state decreed that, beginning in the 1993–1994 school year, high school students must perform seventy-five hours of community service in addition to meeting other academic requirements for graduation. If the Maryland policy is successful, it could soon be adopted in other states as well.

Hard decisions

School-sponsored extracurricular programs exist for the most part because Americans have been willing to support them, either with tax dollars or directly through school fund-raisers and similar activities. Lately, because of rising costs, tight budgets, and other priorities, funds have been harder to come by, and schools are having to cut back on some of the programs they offer.

As this happens, difficult choices must be made. Educators must decide which activities are most beneficial and which activities students can best do without. No national or state guidelines have been set, so decisions are often based on local preference and usually vary from district to district.

Frequently, programs that affect the fewest number of students are the first to go. For instance, programs for exceptionally bright children or for students who need extra help in reading or mathematics may be eliminated. Administrators in Hayward, California, chose to sacrifice a program for a small number of poor readers in order to keep several counselors who could give hundreds of

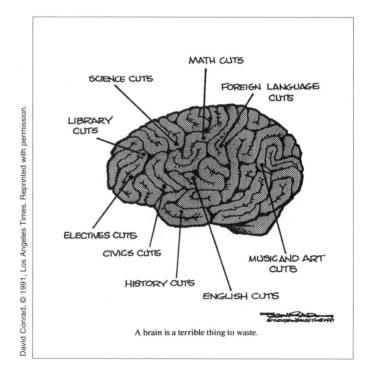

A brain is a terrible thing to waste.

high school seniors advice on careers and college.

Some schools choose to cut sports programs, art classes, and other student activities, believing that those losses will least affect academic performance. Other schools opt to keep student programs but do away with staff positions considered nonessential, such as those of school nurse, counselor, or librarian. Such decisions, however, can draw cries of outrage.

"It [doesn't] add up," says parent Jay Smith of Hatfield, Massachusetts. "How can you have a . . . school, where your beginning of life and learning is books and reading, and you have no library?"

The wisdom of compromise

No parent wants to see his or her child's favorite extracurricular program cut. Still, most people have come to accept the fact that tight budgets will probably force schools to make even more compromises when it comes to both academic and extracurricular programs.

Compromise might be important when it comes to the extras, but it should not be an option when it comes to more essential matters in the education discussion. One of those essentials is teaching. Without exception, highly qualified and creative teachers are necessary in every school if students are to be equipped to meet both today's challenges and those they will be asked to face in the future.

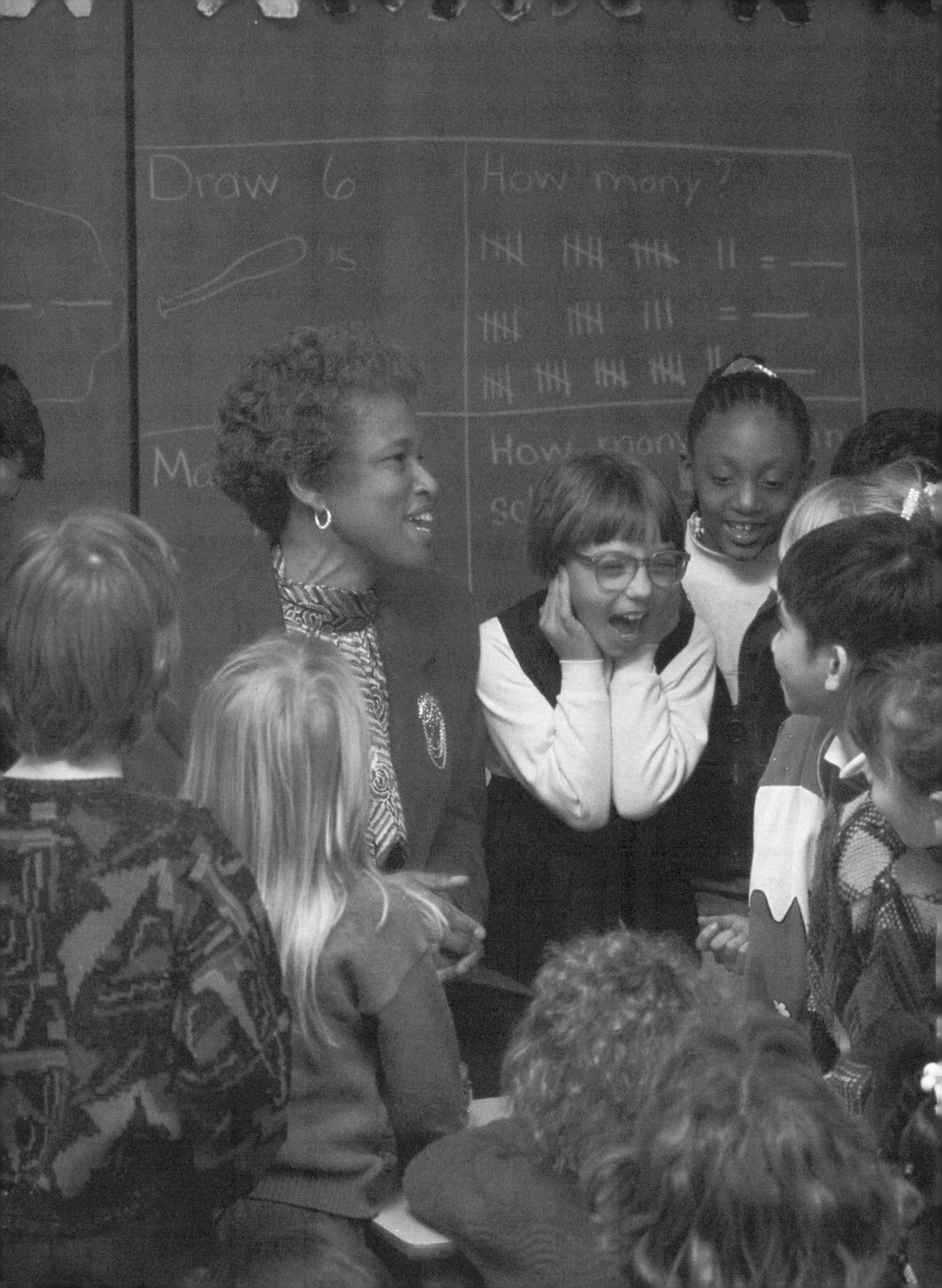
Draw 6
How many?

4

The Task of the Teacher

TEACHERS FACE ENORMOUS challenges in the classroom today. Veteran teachers are often frustrated and weary. Those who are just entering the field are sometimes afraid they will fail to make any significant contributions. In spite of this, however, most teachers share the feelings of Marilyn Grondel, Utah Teacher of the Year for 1990–1991: "Teaching is not a job but involvement in children's lives."

Even enthusiastic teachers like Marilyn Grondel understand that they will be pushed to the limit of their skill and patience when they go to work each day. Students are undisciplined. Administration is demanding. Parents are apathetic. In the face of all this, teachers must stick to lesson plans, maintain a calm and cheerful attitude, and also cope with classroom complications ranging from illiteracy to child abuse, from learning disabilities to a shortage of textbooks. Certainly not all teachers face all of these obstacles. Still, coping with even one or two is often enough to drive many away from the profession.

Managing overly large classes is a widespread challenge facing teachers today. Financially strapped schools are cutting back on the number

(Opposite page) An outstanding teacher has the ability to transform a class assignment into a world adventure. Not all teachers are able to meet the task. Some lack teaching skills while others face obstacles beyond their control.

Small class size allows a teacher to spend more time with each student, addressing his or her special needs.

of teachers they hire and increasing class size to thirty or even forty students. Additionally, many students come to school with special needs. They may be physically or mentally challenged. They may be poor or hungry. They may come from abusive or dysfunctional homes.

Teachers need time if they are to meet all the various needs of their students. Larger classes do not give them that option, as one high school teacher points out in *Teachers at Work:* "I like to get to every kid at least once a period. The periods are forty-eight minutes long, and you have thirty kids. If I get to everybody, I'm not going to hear much from any one person."

Although most educators focus on the benefits to students of small classes, a five-year Tennessee study completed in the 1980s recorded the benefits of a lighter workload for teachers as well. Classes of about twenty children allow teachers to get to know each student more rapidly. Basic instruction can be quickly completed, leaving more time for answering questions, organizing special projects, and working one-on-one with each student. "We know that we can help our students best when we know them as people rather than merely recognize them as faces," explains Jackie E. Swensson, a Colorado educator.

In oversize classes all problems, large and small, are magnified. Teachers find it harder to maintain classroom order and to prevent cheating. They have less time to come up with ways to motivate those who resist learning. High school teachers who sometimes see as many as 150 to 180 students a day become bogged down in piles of uncorrected papers and ungraded reports. Many react by reducing written assignments and cutting back on tests.

"We need fewer students per class period and throughout the school day if we are to teach . . . as responsibly and effectively as we hope to do," says Jackie E. Swensson.

A multitude of languages

All teachers are aware that reading skills are vital in the world today. In spite of having to manage large classes, most teachers are working harder than ever to make sure that every student gets the necessary help in reading. Often, however, students will be at many different reading levels in one classroom. Some are advanced and require challenging material; others need remedial education in order to improve. Particularly with overly large classes, many teachers find that they have little time to meet each student's needs adequately.

The latest arrival of refugees and immigrants into the United States has created an additional challenge to teachers by pouring millions of students who cannot read or even speak English into classrooms across the country. Bilingual programs have been set up, but complications remain. For example, over one hundred languages are spoken by students in California's public schools. Some San Francisco schools express the need for instructors fluent in languages as varied as Spanish, Korean, Polish, Tagalog, and Armenian. In a single midsize elementary school in Virginia in 1989, nineteen different languages were represented, including Arabic, Khmer, Somali, Ga, and Urdu.

Finding teachers who speak these languages can be a long and difficult task. Thus, in many schools, non–English-speaking children are placed in regular classrooms. There, teachers with limited means to communicate with these children must take time from their already crowded schedules to develop alternative means of instruction until these students learn English or can be placed in bilingual classes.

Shortage of supplies

As teachers face challenges ranging from illiteracy to overcrowding, a scarcity of supplies can seem like the last straw. Shortages go beyond equipment such as computers and VCRs. As Susan Moore Johnson writes in her 1990 book *Teachers at Work*, even the basics are at a premium in some schools. For instance, one Massachusetts school was allowed only one pencil per child per year. In another, thirty-five textbooks were shared among 350 students. Gregory Gorbach, who has taught in schools in Ohio, New York, and California, sees the shortages as a national problem. He regularly teaches with no textbooks, simply because many school districts cannot afford them. "Homework is pretty well out of the question," he says. "If I want to give a test, I buy the paper myself."

Gorbach is not the only teacher who spends his own money on supplies for the classroom. Across the country, music teachers buy their own tape

Second graders overflow into the hallway as overcrowding has caused a shortage of desks and supplies.

recorders and music books. Foreign-language teachers purchase audio tapes for language laboratories. Gary Stein, a second-grade teacher in a well-to-do Massachusetts school district, regularly spends "three to four hundred dollars a year on school supplies, school stickers, little books for rewards."

Others cope with the shortage of supplies by making frequent use of the photocopying machine or by relying on PTA fund-raisers to supply needed materials and equipment. PTA support, however, is often not an option in poorer schools where the need is greatest but where parents and the community have no extra funds to channel into schools.

An undervalued profession

To cope with this variety of classroom complications, America needs the best and brightest of teachers in its schools. Teachers are role models; they set the tone and rhythm for all classroom activities. They need to have enthusiasm for what they do. They must know their subjects and know how to present material so students will want to learn. They should be tough but fair and show

Although Americans know the importance of education, the teaching profession gets little respect or support from the general public. Teachers' enthusiasm often diminishes as they must deal with low pay and difficult working conditions.

commitment to their students by being well organized, keeping up on the latest developments in education, and spending extra time with their classes. As educators and authors Terry and Daniel Seymour point out, "In their classrooms is where our children's future is being shaped."

Too often, finding teachers who meet the above qualifications is difficult. At times, locating teachers who just know the basics seems hard to do. In the mid-1980s education experts believed that competency tests would measure the scope of the problem and identify those teachers who needed to improve. The Seymours recorded a portion of the results of those tests in their book *America's Best Classrooms*:

> In Texas . . . over 6,500 [out of 160,000] veteran teachers flunked a basic literacy test. Ten percent of Arkansas teachers failed a math, reading, and

writing exam, while 12 percent of Georgia teachers failed exams in their specific disciplines.

Multiple-choice competency tests have since been found to be poor measurements of such teaching skills as creativity and the ability to work with students. Inferior teachers, however, can be found in almost every school—even those where funds are adequate, students are motivated, and parents support education. If learning takes place, it does so in spite of these educators, not because of them.

Public criticism

Although poor workers are a fact of life in any profession, the public seems particularly critical of teachers. Teachers often get little respect for what they do. Some people blame teachers for all of the problems schools experience. Others think teachers are lazy and enjoy an easy lifestyle—a six-hour workday, summers off, and plenty of holidays. In reality, teachers often spend up to sixty hours a week managing classes, making lesson plans, correcting homework, and leading extracurricular activities.

Says Geraldine Hawes, who teaches English, drama, and speech in a Tennessee high school:

> Anyone who works with students in the performing arts knows about midnight [stage] set building [and] 7:30 AM rehearsals for contest speakers. . . . The term "hard worker" may be trite, but energy, enthusiasm, and a strong work ethic are necessary qualities for a teacher.

Lack of respect, coupled with difficult working conditions, causes many teachers' self-esteem, enthusiasm, and performance to suffer. Some highly motivated and creative college students—those who could make excellent teachers—turn away from teaching to more highly regarded careers. Women, who made up a high percentage of teachers in the past, are rejecting teaching and embracing new options in other careers.

With fewer teachers entering the field, schools have had to hire people who are not fully qualified. This is a particular problem for inner-city schools where conditions are most difficult, challenges are greatest, and pay is poor. For instance, in New York City in 1989 almost thirty-five hundred teachers were hired who had little or no training in education. Even in their first year, few of them received any assistance in the classroom. Their mistakes went uncorrected, and they had to rely on instinct and trial and error when deciding how to lead their classes.

Inadequate training

Hiring poorly prepared educators happens too often in America's schools. Even teachers who have met all requirements necessary for teaching

still may not be adequately trained for the work ahead.

Most teacher-training programs today consist of four years of undergraduate college education. During those four years prospective teachers supposedly get all the training they need in order to perform their future responsibilities in the classroom.

A growing number of educators believe, however, that future teachers would benefit from a fifth year of graduate school that would allow them more time to polish their skills. During that year courses might include training in maintaining discipline in the classroom, inspiring student efforts, communicating with students effectively, and teaching difficult concepts successfully.

Establishing professional standards

Some educators believe that teacher expertise should also be encouraged through the establishment of professional standards. Says Columbia University education professor Linda Darling-Hammond:

> Teaching would be better served by the creation of professional standards boards like those governing other professions, which would establish rigorous and relevant standards of knowledge and meaningful examinations to assess them.

The National Board for Professional Teaching Standards, a newly formed group of teachers and government education officials based in Detroit, Michigan, aims to serve just such a purpose. It argues that board certification—similar to that required for doctors, lawyers, and other professionals—would place a stamp of approval on good teachers and would also inspire other teachers to improve their skills. To encourage colleges and universities to promote excellent teaching, the National Council for Accreditation of Teacher

Education oversees a movement to raise accreditation standards for teacher-training programs. Many formerly accredited schools have had to improve in order to meet tougher professional standards.

Tenure

In order to bring enthusiastic, well-trained teachers into the school system and to sustain high teacher performance over time, legislators and educators are being forced to reevaluate the concept of tenure—the policy by which teachers are guaranteed a permanent position after as few as three years of satisfactory teaching.

Many people believe that tenure is at least partially responsible for the fact that poor teachers remain in America's schools. Tenure protects teachers from getting fired even if they do a poor job. It reduces the chances for young, potentially better-trained educators to get jobs. It makes changes and improvements in teaching more difficult to achieve.

Increasing numbers of lawmakers believe that the time has come to amend or end the tenure policy. Massachusetts focused on the issue in late 1991 when Governor William Weld called for changes that would replace tenure with a recertification procedure to ensure teacher competency. That same year Kentucky school administrators were given the freedom to fire poor teachers if they failed to improve performance in two years. Other states have also begun to examine the wisdom of tenure and are considering alternatives that will be both fair to teachers and helpful for improving education.

Master teachers

Another concept that many educators believe would improve teaching is the creation of the

PERCENTAGE OF SCIENCE EDUCATORS LACKING STATE CERTIFICATION

Source: Council of Chief of State School Officers

STATE	BIOLOGY TEACHERS	CHEMISTRY TEACHERS
CALIFORNIA	18%	17%
FLORIDA	19%	3%
MISSISSIPPI	20%	25%
NEW YORK	8%	7%
SOUTH CAROLINA	8%	6%
NORTH DAKOTA	0%	0%
TOTAL	9%	8%

position of master teacher. Master teachers would be individuals who show great enthusiasm for their subjects. They would communicate well and, through that communication, would inspire other teachers to create more effective teaching programs. They would demand and get excellent performances from their students.

Although there is no nationwide recognition of the position of master teacher, some schools have begun to take the idea seriously. In the mid-1980s Governor Lamar Alexander set up such a program in some Tennessee schools. Master teachers, chosen for their "demonstrated knowledge and actual classroom performance" were then given an increase in salary and asked to train apprentice teachers in that state.

In spite of its public appeal, the idea of master teachers bothers some educators, who point out that many details still need to be worked out. They ask who will judge whether or not a teacher

qualifies to be a master teacher, and what criteria or standards, will be used. They wonder what role teacher unions, which now determine teacher pay and many of the conditions under which teachers work, will play in the creation of master teacher programs in the future.

Higher pay and merit pay

In addition to awarding higher pay for master teachers, raising salaries for all teachers is perhaps the surest way to attract talented educators to schools. In an age when rock stars and sports figures earn millions of dollars a performance, teachers earn very little for the important work they do. Studies show that in 1993 teachers' salaries throughout the United States ranged between twenty and fifty thousand dollars annually, with the average being about thirty-five thousand dollars. Annual salary averages in individual states varied from a low in South Dakota and

Mississippi—slightly over twenty-four thousand dollars—to a high in Connecticut of about forty-eight thousand dollars.

Teachers regularly earn between 25 and 50 percent less than college graduates in other fields. Sometimes they make no more than workers with less education and training. Says veteran teacher Gary Meier of Wisconsin: "Some of my former students, who didn't attend a four-year college and work as technicians for a local utility company, make the same salary after five years as I do after 23 years on the job."

As Meier's situation demonstrates, teachers' salaries not only start low, they remain low. Teachers may reach their peak salary in their mid-thirties, about the time that other professionals are only approaching their prime earning years. With little chance for advancement, many teachers move on to other less demanding or higher income careers just when they have fine-tuned their classroom skills.

People agree that pay raises for all educators would help improve teacher quality. However, the issue of merit pay—extra money for exceptional work—is more controversial. Taxpayers support

Although teachers may enjoy their work, low salaries often force many quality teachers into other higher paying careers.

the idea of higher pay for better performance but are reluctant to fund merit programs. Teachers hesitate to participate in a system that causes them to compete with their colleagues. Administrators, who must develop methods to evaluate teachers, fear that they will become bogged down in paperwork.

Merit systems do work if they are carefully managed, yet singling out teachers for special raises and bonuses has proven to be a divisive measure in many schools in the past decade. Jealousy and hard feelings often spring up between teachers who believe they should have received recognition and those who are actually awarded merit pay. As one teacher interviewed in Susan Moore Johnson's *Teachers at Work* points out, "A lot of people are unhappy with it. They feel that

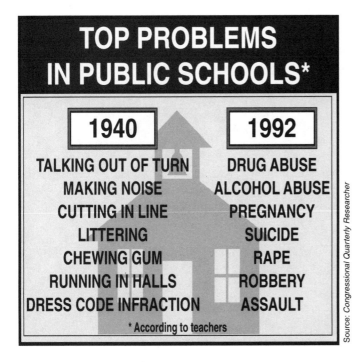

TOP PROBLEMS IN PUBLIC SCHOOLS*

1940	1992
TALKING OUT OF TURN	DRUG ABUSE
MAKING NOISE	ALCOHOL ABUSE
CUTTING IN LINE	PREGNANCY
LITTERING	SUICIDE
CHEWING GUM	RAPE
RUNNING IN HALLS	ROBBERY
DRESS CODE INFRACTION	ASSAULT

* According to teachers

Source: Congressional Quarterly Researcher

they're good teachers, and they don't get merit raises. And the people who have gotten to the top of the scale, they kind of play against each other."

The San Marino Unified School District in California tried and rejected merit pay in the early 1980s. Then-superintendent David Brown said, "[Merit pay] became a moral issue, a teacher issue, a financial issue. . . . It was upsetting the situation that had provided for better programs and instruction."

Increased responsibility and communication

Although teachers are leaders in the classroom, they are often powerless when it comes to overall decision making in their school or district. Teachers have little or no control over who they will teach, the length of the school day, the textbooks they will use, or the way school money is spent. The book *Teachers at Work* tells of one Massachusetts teacher who leads a bilingual class

As teachers spend the majority of their day with their students, there is little time for interaction with other teachers. This isolation keeps teachers from sharing ideas or materials that would be beneficial to their classes.

and was given a computer rather than the supplementary language materials she had requested. The teacher says, "I really don't believe the kids will use the computer in the classroom. I made that clear [to the administration]. I really don't think I need it, but I'm getting it anyway."

This powerlessness often produces frustration in even the best of educators. Their physical presence at school every day makes them expert on how children think and learn, how classes are best taught, and how funds should be allocated. In spite of the skill and experience they have acquired in the classroom, however, their opinions are regularly overlooked or ignored by administrators and lawmakers.

Giving teachers more say in areas where they are most expert would reduce the frustration they feel. As author and educational reformer Ernest Boyer says in *The Great School Debate:*

> I believe this would start the process of building morale, of feeling that [the teachers] matter, that they're a part of the solution and not the problem. It's the attitude of feeling that "I am powerless in this operation" that's causing good people to leave.

Along with increased authority, giving teachers more time to talk to one another about shared concerns could also help reduce frustration and improve performance. Teachers can be virtually isolated in their classrooms. They may see their colleagues only during a lunch break or at the end of a stress-filled day. Rarely do all mathematics teachers or all English teachers have a free hour at the same time so that they can coordinate lessons and ask each other for advice.

Yet, as Marilyn Grondel says in *America's Best Classrooms*, "A successful teacher becomes even more successful by 'dialoguing' with colleagues and sharing ideas and materials." Most teachers seem to agree. In one Gallup poll, over 80 percent of the teachers surveyed testified that sharing ideas and techniques with each other was more valuable than being given their own office or having more staff to help with their paperwork.

Investing in education

In order for the United States to get the educators it needs, it will have to make significant adjustments in the way it looks at the teaching profession. Americans must also realize that teachers alone are not responsible for every problem found in schools.

One area over which they have little control is school finances. Tight budgets have a significant impact—not just on teachers, but on almost every aspect of education. As the push for excellent schools continues, funding has become another noteworthy issue to surface in discussions of reform.

5

Funding for
Better Schools

WITH THE BABY BOOM generation reaching school age in the 1950s, the need for more teachers, more books, and more school buildings increased in the United States. So had the need for education funds. By 1960 the nation's bill for schools stood at about $15.5 billion, with new projects to help educate poor and minority students promising to send the total even higher. In the 1970s and 1980s educators pointed out the need for computers in classrooms, better pay for teachers, programs to help children with special needs, and improved school security. By 1993 total education costs, public and private, for the nation topped $490 billion.

People accepted those rising costs, believing they were necessary for better schools. But when education did not appear to improve—test scores remained level or dropped, high school graduates failed to qualify for jobs—people realized that money was not solving all of the nation's education problems. In many cases money was being wasted, thrown away on programs that did not work and on administrators and staff who did not make students and their education a top priority.

73

By the 1980s the willingness to pay for the high price of education was declining. As Robert Lundeen, cochairman of the Task Force on Education for Economic Growth observed in 1983:

> I don't believe that any taxpayers, faced with the burdens that all of them have these days, are going to be very enthusiastic about increasing the revenue for schools unless they're convinced that what already is being spent is being spent effectively.

Today Americans view the high cost of education with continued skepticism. They hear about the growing problems in schools—bureaucratic mismanagement, lack of discipline, drugs, gangs, and violence—and are reluctant to vote for bond issues and levies, or taxes, for fear that the money will be wasted. Some older citizens prefer to put their money into retirement and health-care programs and let the parents of students support schools. Businesspeople, coping with high business costs and troubled economies, oppose increased education funding because they know that higher taxes will cut profits.

Inequalities in funding

When it comes to funding schools, only a little over 50 percent of necessary money is provided by state and federal governments. The rest comes, as it always has, from local property taxes levied, or imposed, on landowners in individual school districts. Although property taxes provided enough money to support all schools adequately in the past, today they do not. Wealthy and middle-class Americans have moved out of the cities and into the suburbs, taking their tax dollars with them. The poor, unable to afford homes in the well-to-do suburbs, have been left in deteriorating inner-city neighborhoods where homes are older and property tax revenues low.

Schools in poor neighborhoods are continually in economic difficulties. Funds are not available to build new buildings, hire good teachers, or buy new textbooks. Vandalism and violence have increased the need for maintenance, security guards, and metal detectors, all of which cost money. To meet these costs, lawmakers have hiked property tax rates on inner-city residents. As a result, poor families pay a higher percentage of their income in property taxes than do wealthy families. That money, however, is still far less than the amount spent on suburban schools.

Educators such as Jonathan Kozol charge that inequalities in school funding have continued in part because of the isolation of inner cities and in part because of racial inequality. Kozol points out that the great majority of inner-city parents are poorly educated minorities, unfamiliar with how

Students from Richard Rogers Elementary School in New York play in front of graffiti-covered buildings. Poor school districts often lack the funds to keep their schools properly maintained.

to make their needs known and unlikely to vote in elections. Lawmakers and school administrators have, for the most part, ignored their needs and responded instead to middle-class parents who are more verbal and more likely to vote for those who support suburban schools.

The lack of equality between schools in affluent and low-income areas can be dramatic. Wealthy school districts in states such as Kentucky could spend over four thousand dollars a student in 1989, while poor districts made do with seventeen hundred dollars. In 1993 New Jersey's well-to-do districts allocated almost eight thousand dollars a pupil, while its poorest districts allotted about six thousand dollars.

In an effort to equalize support, many states legislated funding levels so that all schools would receive at least the minimum amount of money needed to educate children. More often than not, however, the guaranteed support was still far from adequate. Citizens in wealthier school districts boosted funding by voting to pay higher property taxes. Financially strapped parents could not contribute this extra money, even though schools in their districts were ones that would most benefit from an additional source of funds.

Government funding

Although schools have a legitimate need for increased funding, state governments have had to cut back on education support in the 1990s because of tight budgets, taxpayer rebellions, and other spending priorities. Troubles that included a drought, military cutbacks, and a recession caused California governor Pete Wilson to request a suspension of the law that decrees that 40 percent of state moneys must go to education. Across the country similar cutbacks resulted in larger classes, lower teacher salaries, and inferior programs for students.

If states cannot provide funding, educators hope that the federal government will. Because only about 6 percent of total education money comes from Washington, D.C., many people consider that increased federal support for education is long overdue.

In the past, federal funds have gone toward special programs such as Head Start, initiated in the 1960s to prepare poor and at-risk youngsters for school. Even these programs, however, have been chronically limited by a lack of money. Many eligible children never received help.

In spite of their stated concern for education, Presidents Ronald Reagan and George Bush put little emphasis on increasing federal funds for schools. In 1992 Congress allocated a total of about $30 billion for education, with emphasis again on programs for the disabled and disadvantaged. That amount was only a little over 2 percent of total federal spending for the year. By comparison, amounts set aside for defense in 1992 stood at $290 billion, while moneys used to save hundreds of failing savings and loans surpassed $150 billion.

These preschoolers are part of the Head Start program. Although Congress allocated funding for education of disadvantaged children, the Head Start program remains financially strapped.

With the future of millions of young Americans at stake, many people want to make education funding a top priority of the federal government. President Clinton seems to support those wishes and included in his 1995 budget request a 7 percent increase in education funding—an additional $1.7 billion. "This request . . . is a clear sign of the president's commitment and resolve to invest in children and youth—our future," says Secretary of Education Richard Riley. Critics, however, fear that money will be cut from other programs or that funds may run short when programs are finally under way.

Lotteries and education

Some states struggling to find money for education and other programs have turned to legalized gambling in an attempt to solve their funding shortages. In 1963 New Hampshire established the first legal lottery to operate in the United States since the 1890s. Other state governments soon realized that revenues could be produced from this source and established their own lotteries. By 1992 annual income from lotteries nation-

In downtown Chicago a line forms to purchase lottery tickets. Although lotteries were created to generate extra money for the state, their effect on education has been minimal.

wide reached $11.5 billion. In 1993 thirty-seven states, plus the District of Columbia, were making use of authorized lotteries.

Although lotteries bring in extra money, their overall effect on education funding is disappointing. In most of the thirteen states where lotteries were established specifically to help public schools, funding for education has not increased significantly. In many cases legislators merely substitute lottery money for education funds. And because many Americans believe that lotteries are supplying additional funds for schools, they vote down badly needed levies and bond issues.

"The public is now reluctant to pass education bond issues because they think we're floating in lottery money," says former California state school superintendent Bill Honig.

Demands to equalize fundings

As an awareness of school funding inequalities grew in the late 1980s, however, some parents and educators in financially poor districts took steps that they hoped would eventually improve their schools. Movements began in Montana, Kentucky, and Texas, where state supreme courts were called on to review school finance laws. The plaintiffs maintained that using property taxes to fund schools was unfair, principally because poor districts raised fewer taxes than wealthy ones and, therefore, had less money to spend on students.

The first decision was handed down in June 1989, when the Kentucky Supreme Court ruled against the state's reliance on property taxes to support education. "Kentucky's entire system of [public] schools is unconstitutional," wrote Chief Justice Robert F. Stephens. The court required Kentucky lawmakers to rethink school funding to make it more equitable. Within the next several years other courts ruled in a similar manner. By

1992 twenty-three states faced lawsuits that cited funding gaps as a cause for inequalities between rich and poor schools.

With orders to change, state legislators began looking for ways to provide funding that would be equal and adequate. Most chose to use a combination of property taxes and other taxes to bring in additional money. For instance, Montana legislated an extra 5 percent individual income tax to raise additional money for schools. Kentucky increased sales tax and corporate taxes. New Jersey opted for higher sales, income, and excise taxes.

Change in Texas has proven more difficult. In 1989 the Texas Supreme Court ruled that the state must somehow narrow the difference between the nine thousand dollars per pupil per year available in some wealthy districts and the slightly over three thousand dollars per student per year being raised in poor ones.

The following year the Texas legislature voted to provide more funds for poor districts by raising sales and cigarette taxes. In September 1990 a lower court declared that that reform was not adequate and gave legislators a year to come up with a better plan. Two more proposals—both based on transferring property taxes from rich to poor districts—were rejected as well. Work on an acceptable plan continues, with the state passing stopgap, or temporary, funding measures that allow schools to continue to operate.

The Michigan plan

Not the courts, but a crisis in the Kalkaska School District in 1993 helped convince the state of Michigan to make changes in the way it financed education. Residents of Kalkaska, a northwest Michigan town, had three times defeated a property tax increase that educators claimed was necessary to keep schools operating.

Still, no one expected school officials to announce in March of that year that summer vacation was starting almost immediately because of a lack of funds. Classes wound up with a rush. Plans and expectations were turned topsy-turvy. High school senior Matt Johnston, who hoped to complete an advanced-placement calculus class and earn college credits, said, "The [nationwide calculus] test is in May, but no one [here] is prepared to take it."

As Kalkaska schools closed amid complaints from parents and much ado in the press, lawmakers decided the time had come to act. To avoid a continuation of funding problems that had plagued the state for years, they came up with a plan to do away with property taxes as a source of school money and replace them with funds from a 2 percent sales tax hike and an increase in cigarette taxes. In March 1994 voters approved the new plan. The decision was a historic one for the nation.

"One thing is clear. A more equitable and stable method of financing public schools must be found, and Michigan has clearly taken a bold step in that direction," says Ernest Boyer of the Carnegie Foundation.

Nationwide debate

Because of its boldness, the plan caused a commotion among parents, educators, and lawmakers across the country. Some were interested in getting the details. Others were quick to point out potential weaknesses, including the fact that sales taxes affect poor people as much as or more than the well-to-do, and that spending slumps will produce lower school revenues. As Raymond Mackey of the American Federation of Teachers warned, "There will be fiscal problems in the future. That's not a warning but a fact."

Michigan was not the first state where a refusal by citizens to pay higher taxes has had an impact on education. In 1978 California residents passed Proposition 13, a measure that reduced property tax income by $7 billion. The cut, coupled with a flood of immigrants entering the state, placed enormous strain on public schools. Many now face bankruptcy. Conditions have caused some parents to turn to private schools.

In some states tax protests come from well-to-do people who rebel at paying higher taxes to educate other people's children. For instance, after Democratic governor James Florio of New Jersey supported a $2 billion tax increase in 1990—much of which was earmarked for poorer school districts in the state—property owners expressed their outrage by voting out the Democratic majority in the legislature.

The public's concern with the so-called Robin Hood approach—taking from the rich to give to the poor—is expressed by the school superinten-

A sign posted in front of a Los Angeles house advocates passage of Proposition 13. California voters passed this measure in 1978. It reduced property taxes but has also strained the public school system.

dent of one wealthy district in New Jersey. In an October 1991 article in *Time*, the superintendent says: "The point of reform was to make all schools quality schools. But I fear that everything will settle into mediocrity."

Poor schools usually have a greater need for supplies, maintenance, and attention than wealthier ones, making fair distribution of public money a difficult task.

Helping one helps all

Education experts point out that Americans should not fear that helping poor school districts will automatically hurt affluent ones. The United States is a wealthy country, with plenty of resources available to make education equal and excellent for all.

Despite the voices raised to protest the changes, the move to equalize funding of schools seems to be under way. For those who wish to continue to be heard, another issue offers them the opportunity to be involved in school reform. That issue is choice, and it is one of the broadest and most challenging that schools face today.

6

Schools and Choice

UNTIL RECENTLY MOST Americans took little interest in the issues and problems that schools face. Instead, they let school administrators make decisions about policy and funding and trusted that children would get the best education possible as a result.

Today, it is a well-known fact that schools do not always do a good job of educating. The reasons are diverse, but some people believe that they can be linked to a single, underlying cause: the fact that most people do not have enough influence over schools. Specifically, parents have little choice about which schools their children attend. Some believe that, if given this option, parents would become more involved, schools would be accountable to parental demands, and education for all students would improve.

Whether it proves to be the answer to school shortcomings or not, choice is growing in popularity. Parents consider options for their children that range from publicly funded private schools to home schooling, from profit-making schools to charter and magnet schools. All possibilities have

(Opposite page) With the various problems plaguing America's schools, many parents would like to have greater influence over their child's schooling.

their strengths and their drawbacks. All deserve consideration if America is serious about renewing its troubled education system.

Competition and choice

There is a growing belief that American schools would improve if they were operated as businesses. Like businesses, those schools that do not produce a quality product—that is, education—at a price that satisfies the customer—parents and students—would either improve or shut down. Those schools that trim the fat out of budgets, pare down management, hire competent employees, and come up with a quality education for their students would flourish.

As author and editor Peter Brimelow says, "[Public education's] problems will remain chronic until it is exposed to competition. That is a proposition [businesspeople] can easily understand."

For this competitive spirit to develop in the education field, parents must be able to have a choice about where their children attend school. The idea attracted nationwide attention when President George Bush proposed that the government help parents pay private school tuition.

President George Bush gives students from St. Peter's Interparish School a tour of the White House. During his presidency, Bush advocated government help for parents who wish to send their children to private schools.

"It's time parents were free to choose the schools that their children attend," Bush said in April 1991. "This approach will create the competitive climate that stimulates excellence in our private [nonreligious] and parochial [religious] schools as well."

The unveiling of the Bush proposal opened the way for discussions about choice across the country. Some districts already had limited choice plans, and those came under close scrutiny. People began to realize that choice means different things to different people.

For parents in Cambridge, Massachusetts, choice has been fairly limited. Beginning in 1981 parents could name their first, second, and third choice of district schools in which they wished to enroll their children. Only public schools were included, and restrictions regarding space and racial balance existed as well.

Other districts have given choice a wider meaning. Beginning in 1990 Minnesota students could enroll in any public school in the state, with parents required to provide transportation, and again taking into consideration space and racial balance. Fewer than 1 percent of families have opted to take this opportunity for change, but educators consider the program a success, since these students have expressed greater satisfaction with their schools, and some dropouts have returned to classes.

Concerns of educators

Despite growing support for competition and choice, many educators are still skeptical. They wonder how American parents will get adequate information about schools so they can make good choices. Perhaps schools will have to advertise, using funds that would otherwise go for books and teachers' salaries. Perhaps parents will have to visit a large number of schools, interviewing teachers and evaluating the quality of education offered. If so, how would parents know what to look for, and what would happen to students whose parents did not bother to specify a school? As education consultant David Thornburg points out:

> My concern is that parents are not, on the average, any more expert on education than the public at large. . . . I know a great many parents who would keep their kids out of school to babysit siblings. I would suggest that [few] parents know about the educational needs of the next century.

Many parents, legislators, and educators seem willing to take the risk. In 1989 Arkansas, Arizona, Iowa, Nebraska, and Ohio voted to allow some degree of choice in their public school systems. In 1990 Washington and Idaho did the same. Other states wait to see if the policy significantly improves education before they act.

Private schools for public education

Although a significant number of Americans support the concept of choice, they question President Bush's proposal to include private schools in the country's definition of public education. According to Bush:

> Whether a school is organized by privately financed educators or town councils or religious orders or denominations, any school that serves the public and is held accountable by the public authority provides public education.

Private schools, however, are not actually held accountable to a public authority. They set their own standards and decide for themselves what they are going to teach and how they are going to teach it. Neither are they supported by taxes, but by private donations or student tuition.

Apart from concerns about funding private schools with public money, the popularity of private schools has grown in recent years. Their

Private schools often have smaller classes than public schools, allowing more interaction between teachers and students.

numbers increased by 30 percent during the 1980s. In 1992 more than 4.8 million students attended private schools that range from parochial, or religious, academies run by Catholics, Lutherans, Methodists, and Jews to preparatory schools, where students prepare for entrance into colleges and universities.

The attraction of private schools is not difficult to understand. The quality and safety of many public schools have been questioned in past years. In private schools class sizes are smaller and expectations are higher. Discipline can be strict. Parents who take the trouble to place their children in private schools are usually more supportive and involved, creating a more cooperative atmosphere within the school.

Vouchers

Many parents who want to send their children to private schools are unable to because of the cost. In order to make private schools affordable and give all Americans a real choice of schools, the Bush administration proposed that a voucher system be created. Vouchers—government certificates worth several thousand dollars—would be

" . . . One nation, under God, indivisible . . . "

Drawingboard. Reprinted by permission of Paul Duginski.

issued to all parents who could then use them to pay for their children's public or private education.

Wisconsin was the first state to experiment with a voucher plan. In 1991 low-income parents received twenty-five hundred dollars in state-funded vouchers to pay for attendance at any nonreligious private school. About one thousand students qualified for the plan, but fewer than four hundred actually changed schools because only a small number of private schools chose to participate in the experiment.

Few other states had tried vouchers when Californians were asked to vote on a voucher proposal in 1993. The proposal would have allowed parents to enroll their children in any public or private school of their choice in the state. The vote was seen as a test case for the nation. If residents in a state where public schools were chronically overcrowded and underfunded expressed confidence in vouchers, so might citizens in other states. On the other hand, if Californians rejected the plan, the future of public support for private schools might be in jeopardy.

The proposal had numerous critics. Many believed that using vouchers to pay for private schools would further weaken California's already troubled public school system. Parents would take money that once went to public schools and invest it in private schools of their choice. People believed that students who stayed in public schools would end up getting an even poorer education than they did before.

Some predicted that as the demand for private schools increased, tuition could rise, and vouchers would no longer cover the costs. Poor students would have to return to public schools that would no longer have the funds to serve them. Others argued that in America separation of church and state would make government funding through the voucher system of religious private schools unconstitutional.

When it came to a vote in California, the majority sided with the critics, and the proposal failed. Because neither President Clinton nor Education Secretary Richard Riley support vouchers, the issue has slipped from the national agenda—at least for the time being.

Magnet schools

With the debate over public money for private schools put on hold, interest in new variations of public schooling has grown. One of the most popular options is the magnet school. Magnet schools may be self-contained facilities or schools within schools—part of other school campuses. They are created with the purpose of drawing bright and highly motivated students to their programs. As alternatives to more traditional schools, they are attractive because teachers and students work together in small groups and thus have opportunities to share common interests and experiment with nontraditional learning techniques.

In magnet schools curriculum is specialized. Many of the approximately five thousand magnet schools across the country concentrate on mathematics, science, foreign languages, or the arts, but there are exceptions. The Center for International Commerce in Long Beach, California, prepares

Secretary of Education Richard Riley strongly supported an overhaul of the nation's schools but opposed the voucher proposal.

Students at work in the Downtown Kindergarten Magnet in St. Paul, Minnesota. Magnet schools such as this one are open to students of all races and economic levels.

high school graduates for careers in international relations and global business. City Magnet School in Lowell, Massachusetts, teaches traditional classes every morning then allows students to manage and take part in a society of their own creation every afternoon. During that time they learn mathematics by working and paying taxes (using play money), study law by carrying out mock trials, and understand politics by holding classroom elections.

Critics point out that magnet schools are basically unfair to the vast majority of students. "[They] reward top talent, pure and simple," says educator Braughn Taylor. Magnets are more expensive than ordinary schools. In addition, they pull the best teachers from traditional classrooms, leaving students there to make do with less talented leadership.

On the other hand, magnet schools are open to students of all races and economic levels, and thus they can be real avenues to success for disadvantaged students. Some magnets, such as the Environmental Technology Academy in Philadelphia, Pennsylvania, emphasize vocational skills and include average students who are willing to work hard and attend school regularly.

In magnet schools attendance is high, often above 96 percent. Magnets graduate more than their share of National Merit scholarship winners, and student test scores are exceptional. Six years after Lowell's City Magnet School opened its doors in 1981, its students tested two years above national norms in reading and mathematics. By 1990 thirteen eighth graders passed first-year college-level examinations in those same subjects. Educators have also found that the presence of a magnet program on a traditional campus can produce a halo effect, encouraging students in traditional classes to perform better.

Charter schools

Another aspect of choice and reform that has gained favorable attention in recent years is the concept of charter schools—schools operated by private individuals or groups who have been chartered, or authorized by the state, to run them. Charter schools can be set up by teachers, by colleges, by businesses, or by organizations such as zoos and museums. For instance, in Massachusetts, Boston University runs the school system in the nearby town of Chelsea. In Chicago a group of corporations manages a tuition-free model elementary school. Charter schools are often supported by a combination of public funds and tuition. In most cases education, not profit, is their priority.

Many educators are enthusiastic about charter schools because they involve less regulation and waste than is often found in public school

Charter schools such as the Corporate/Community Schools in Chicago often tailor their educational programs to the needs of students in the community.

bureaucracies. Like magnet schools, most charter facilities are specialized in some way, and education is tailored to the needs of students. For instance, one charter school may teach hearing-impaired students. Another focuses on students interested in the arts. One Los Angeles charter school, Edutrain, educates troubled or homeless teens. Because Edutrain students must deal with the effects of problems such as drugs, gangs, and crime, class hours are flexible, child care is provided, and courses offer practical information that can be applied to daily life. The school was originally part of the Los Angeles School District, but Edutrain directors now set their own rules, which range from the kinds of teachers they hire to the number of credits students need for graduation.

Several groups of lawmakers have already passed bills that authorize the creation of charter schools in their states. In 1991 Minnesota became the first state in the nation to enact a charter school law. It now allows the formation of up to twenty charter schools to be operated by state-certified educators. California's law, passed in 1992, allows one hundred charter schools to operate.

Critics fear that charters could permit unqualified people to operate schools. Supporters, however, point out that charters give parents choice, grant teachers greater opportunities to educate creatively, and—perhaps most importantly—make students a top priority.

Schools for profit

One variation of charter schools—the for-profit school—may have something other than the students' education as its main interest. Many people fear that companies that view education as a source of profit may lose sight of students' learning in the scramble to make as much money as possible.

THE FOLLY OF FOR-PROFIT SCHOOLS

Companies that operate for profit can create and manage schools independently from the public school system, or they can be hired to run troubled public schools more efficiently. Perhaps the most widely publicized venture is the Edison Project, headed by businessperson Christopher Whittle.

Whittle is known for his controversial Channel One network that broadcasts news and educational programs laced with advertising to thousands of schools every day. In 1992 he announced the formation of the Edison Project, through which he planned to build a chain of profit-making schools that would eventually serve two million students across the nation. "The motive of profit and the motive for public good are not mutually exclusive. We are a private institution with a public mission," said Whittle in 1992.

Whittle claimed that his schools would provide an excellent, low-cost education by cutting administrative costs, using parents as volunteers, and replacing some teachers with closed-circuit television and other high-tech methods of

At Gahr High School in Cerritos, California, an advanced placement English class watches a Channel One broadcast.

instruction. Some experts, however, questioned his calculations, given the fact that he would be faced with building construction and start-up costs.

Their skepticism seemed well founded. In 1993, because of a shortage of funds, the project was scaled back. Whittle announced that he would reform existing schools that asked for his help rather than build schools from the ground up. Following this new plan, by the spring of 1994 Whittle had succeeded in signing contracts to run three Massachusetts elementary schools. He remains optimistic that he will be involved in operating schools in other states in the near future.

For-profit schooling successes

Another private corporation, a Minneapolis-based firm called Educational Alternatives, Inc. (EAI), has become known for two profit-making schools it established in the late 1980s. In 1990 school administrators in south Dade County, Florida, hired the company to manage a newly built public school there. The venture was reportedly successful, resulting in enthusiastic parents, contented teachers, and motivated students. Favorable publicity led EAI to a contract with the city of Baltimore in 1992 to oversee nine inner-city schools there.

Observers feared that the company would have trouble making a profit in Baltimore, where school buildings were decrepit, technologies outdated, and teachers suspicious of change. After more than a year under new management, however, the district seems satisfied. "They are doing everything they were pledged to do," says Baltimore school superintendent Walter Amprey.

EAI took on an even greater challenge in October 1994, when school officials in Hartford, Connecticut, voted to hire the company to run the

Entrepreneur Christopher Whittle forged a union between education and profit making with his Channel One broadcasts and Edison Project.

entire school district, a total of thirty-two schools. Hartford is one of the poorest cities in Connecticut. Its students have some of the highest drop-out rates and lowest test scores in the state.

As other private-education companies appear on the scene, many people remain uneasy about the profit-making rationale. They worry that if profits fail to materialize, quality of education will decline, or, even worse, schools will close. In cases where neighborhood public schools have been privatized, or made private, children could then be left with no schools to attend at all.

Home schooling

While some parents are intent on reforming the public school system, others decide that home schooling best meets the needs of their family. The U.S. Department of Education estimates that

A math teacher from Hartford, Connecticut, displays a sign in protest of the proposal to allow EAI, a private corporation, to manage the city's schools.

some 350,000 children were schooled at home in the 1990s, compared to only 15,000 in the early 1980s. And although many educators worry that children may receive inferior education at home, a 1990 study shows that home-schooled children scored higher in mathematics, reading, science, language, and social studies than 80 percent of their peers taught in traditional classrooms.

Many parents favor home schooling because it provides a setting in which their children can learn without being exposed to negative social issues that exist in many schools today. Home schooling also allows parents the greatest chance for involvement in their children's education. It gives them opportunities to teach personal values and provides enormous flexibility when it comes to curriculum and scheduling. For instance, a trip to the grocery store could be used as a lesson in practical arithmetic as well as a chance to

Increasing numbers of parents are pulling their children out of public schools and teaching them at home. A New Hampshire woman goes over a lesson at home with her four children.

practice wise decision making in the marketplace.

"Courses in the home school could lead children into the garden to study botany, or to the local zoo to study zoology," points out University of Pittsburgh researcher Jane Avner.

Many Americans are critical of home schooling for several reasons. First, some families lack the necessary self-discipline. Telephone calls, television, younger siblings, and a host of other interruptions can easily disrupt study times. Secondly, parents often lack skills necessary to teach more difficult subjects such as foreign languages, higher mathematics, and laboratory sciences. Finally, students who study at home miss out on many opportunities for social development that they would regularly get at school. They do not have as many chances to learn independence, leadership, and teamwork, gain problem-solving skills, make friends, or deal with aggression.

Most of these shortcomings are easily overcome, however. Educational supplements—home chemistry lab kits, foreign-language tapes, and community art classes—can be used to enhance texts and parental instruction. Extracurricular activities such as church groups, service clubs, and team sports provide opportunities for home-schooled children to interact with their peers.

Making the choices

Among the multitude of reforms being made in education today, private schools, magnet schools, charter schools, and for-profit schools are only some of the options being tried. Independent projects such as the Coalition of Essential Schools, founded in 1984 by former Harvard University dean Theodore R. Sizer, continually work for improvement. The coalition encourages participating schools to concentrate on essentials such as lowering teacher workloads and viewing the student as a worker rather than a receiver of information.

The National Alliance for Restructuring Education and other similar groups work to create partnerships between businesses, such as Apple Computer and Xerox Corporation, and schools that can benefit from such support. Projects supported by teacher associations and other education organizations are also working hard for reform.

Schools are rapidly changing, and more change is on the way. Author and government adviser David Osborne, writing in the September 1993 issue of *Mother Jones,* comments:

> If you look at everything that's going on around the country and put it all together, you realize that our public-education system in ten years is going to look radically different than it looked ten years ago.

It is hoped that change will lead to better-educated students. If not, other alternatives may hold the key to improvement for schools of the future.

7

Schools for the Future

THE 1983 LANDMARK REPORT *A Nation at Risk* reminded educators that schools cannot be unchanging institutions, ignoring changes in the world, insisting on doing business in the same old way. A decade later concerned and creative educators and parents have shown that there is a multitude of new ways to look at education. Ideas for reform are surfacing every year. Only time will tell if the experiments will prove successful. In the meantime a growing number of people agree that the country as a whole needs to define the goals and standards it wants for its schools. As Secretary of Education Richard Riley says:

> If this country is to have a great future we're going to have to connect the generation . . . now in the public schools to learning in a much more significant way. The first step is to define what learning is and what students are expected to learn and be able to do.

National standards

Passage of the Goals 2000: Educate America Act and the creation of the National Education Standards and Improvement Council in 1994 were two of the first steps taken by the federal

(Opposite page) Students must be well versed in math, history, science, English, geography, and computer technology if they are to successfully face the challenges of the future.

government to develop a set of national standards for education in the United States. Although the actual creation of standards is voluntary and will be the responsibility of each state, the council will examine and approve goals if and when they are submitted. At least thirty-four states have created or are creating standards for their schools.

The federal government is not alone in working on standards. Among several other projects, the New Standards Project is an association of nineteen states and several school districts headed by the National Center on Education and the Economy in Rochester, New York, and the Learning Research and Development Center at the University of Pittsburgh in Pennsylvania. The project offers guidance on standard setting, provides course outlines and exam materials, and allows schools to share information, thus encouraging uniformity. Other organizations such as the National Center for History in the Schools and the National Academy of Sciences are defining standards in such fields as history and science.

As the process of developing standards continues, experts agree that everyone—teachers, principals, parents, and students—should be included in discussions. Many concerns need to be addressed.

Local concern over national standards

Some people worry that the federal government's involvement will threaten local control of education. "Heretofore [previously], the federal role has been in funding . . . programs for special needs. With this [standards project the government] moved into the area of general education," says Michael Resnick of the National School Boards Association. Others fear that minority and disadvantaged students will be shortchanged or overlooked. Says Glen Cutlip of the National Education Association:

We seriously question the ability of the current educational system to make [quality education] a reality for all children, given the inadequate and unequal distribution of resources, the lack of technological innovation and the lack of flexibility for change.

The formation of opportunity-to-learn standards could satisfy that concern. These standards would compel, or force, states to provide extra funding for disadvantaged schools. Some states already have such legislation on their books; others do not.

A major concern is that standards will result in a vast number of rules, as happened in Ohio, where teachers were faced with more than two hundred specific reading objectives for students. Proponents of standards emphasize that they are working for guidelines for education, not a national curriculum that dictates every detail of learning. States and school districts will still be responsible for choosing textbooks, courses, and teachers, and they will be encouraged to keep objectives, or goals, general.

"It's a great thing if kids emerge with the basics and freedom to broaden their frontiers," says William H. Kolberg, a businessperson involved in the standards project. "How to do this for all kids is tough, but this is the first time we have a national strategy for change."

Testing and portfolios

Those who believe that national standards will improve education also feel that new types of tests to measure improvement will be necessary. A reliance on tests is common in most industrialized countries and is especially popular in the United States. American students are subjected to a variety of tests designed to measure readiness, achievement, and intelligence. According to one report 46 million students from kindergarten

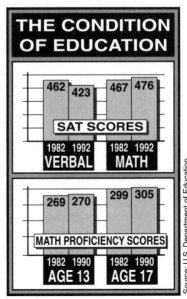

THE CONDITION OF EDUCATION

462 423 467 476

SAT SCORES

1982 1992   1982 1992
VERBAL   MATH

269 270   299 305

MATH PROFICIENCY SCORES

1982 1990   1982 1990
AGE 13   AGE 17

Source: U.S. Department of Education

through high school are given more than 100 million such tests annually.

Most of these are computerized and multiple-choice. Many educators feel that this type of examination not only carries a built-in bias that handicaps minorities and other groups, but that it fails to measure factors such as persistence, creativity, and effort. As education reformer Theodore Sizer points out, "You cannot test intellectual habits."

In order to gain a more complete measure of how well a student is learning, many educators suggest the creation of portfolios, similar to those put together by artists. For instance, an English portfolio might include examples of a student's poems, essays, and other assignments that would demonstrate creativity and communication skills.

While portfolios would be valuable in areas such as languages, arts, and sciences, creating a mathematics portfolio might be more difficult. "We still don't know what a math portfolio should be," admits Ann Rainey, an award-winning Vermont elementary teacher whose school began a pilot portfolio program several years ago. Another difficulty waiting to be solved is how to create a fair and practical system to grade portfolios.

New approaches to education

National standards can encourage excellence in education, but they may do little to remedy ills such as overburdened teachers, uninvolved families, and poorly motivated students. Some educators believe that the answers to these kinds of problems will be found in new approaches to education that have not yet been well explored in the United States.

One possibility has been dubbed "the parallel school" by author and historian James M. Banner Jr. The parallel school would be separate from traditional schools and would be scheduled after regular school hours. It would provide services such as counseling, driver education, drug-abuse programs, and after-school sports that ordinary public schools today now struggle to include in their overcrowded schedules. Schools could then be responsible for academic courses alone, giving teachers and students time to concentrate on the traditional academic subjects.

The parallel school remains an untested project, but other education alternatives are being tried in a limited way in some parts of the country. For instance, satellite schools—public schools located within buildings that house large businesses or corporations—are being tried in Miami, Florida. The purpose of these facilities is to encourage bonding between schools and businesses and to give working parents the opportunity to become more involved in their children's education and lives.

Gradeless classes, in which early elementary students are grouped by ability rather than age, have been in existence in some Kentucky schools since 1990. Educators hope this type of class will help prevent underachievers from being promoted from grade to grade. Experts predict that the new format will produce improvements in student learning and increased student self-esteem.

Educators in Baltimore, Maryland, believe that single-sex education could also be important for education in the future, despite the fact it has the potential to encourage division between the sexes. Baltimore teachers who lead all-male classrooms in high-crime communities testify that they are better able to concentrate on specific behavior problems and learning weaknesses.

Single-sex classes may also help reduce poor self-esteem that causes some girls to lag behind boys in mathematics and science skills when they reach their high school years. Says Barbara E. Wagner, head of Marlborough School, a single-sex facility for girls in the Los Angeles area:

> I believe (single-sex education) has afforded young women the opportunities . . . to become leaders, outstanding academicians, including in math and science. . . . The girls here feel very competent. They dream big dreams, and they see anything is possible for them.

Personalized curriculum

As schools of the future become more aware of individual student needs, independent education programs (IEPs) may become an important part of the learning process. IEPs, originally developed around 1975, require educators to evaluate the needs of students with learning and physical disabilities and prepare plans that specifically meet their learning needs. These plans are reviewed and adjusted regularly so that students receive the best education possible.

Some educators believe that schools of tomorrow will provide all students with such individualized plans. For instance, students who have trouble reading but do well in mathematics will be given remedial help in the former and enrichment, or accelerated, courses in the latter. As more schools allow children to learn at their own pace, IEPs will become valuable tools for keeping track of students' progress.

High-tech learning

The increasing availability of high-technology equipment in schools promises to make the creation of IEPs practical as well as beneficial. Instead of putting individualized programs together by hand for each student, educators will be able to turn to computerized programs to create lesson plans and track student progress.

Technology will make learning easier and more enjoyable in other ways as well. Students will use school computers to locate supplemental material they might overlook or avoid in a traditional library. Software programs such as one already offered by IBM will allow students to read a passage from a novel, call up a panel of experts to comment on and explain the text, and then

Schools of the future will utilize computer software programs to personalize education. Likewise, students will be able to access information and supplemental materials via the computer.

access information about the related period of history they are studying.

Although the initial cost of such technology will be too expensive for some schools, later savings could be significant. Computers, videos, and virtual reality programming can be used in place of field trips and science laboratories, eliminating travel expenses and costly equipment. This type of technology might also be used to meet the needs of students in remote areas who have few chances to visit museums, concert halls, technology centers, and other resources.

Parental involvement

A greater emphasis on parental involvement will undoubtedly be another feature of education in the future. Multiple studies have shown that no matter what the educational or economic level of a family, children do better if their parents take an active role in their education. Some parents may only ensure that homework is completed on time. Others will volunteer in classrooms, or become part of site-based management teams. The National PTA is working to make sure that all elementary and secondary schools have strong parental involvement programs set up by the year 2000.

"[Parents] will be able to participate in developing and knowing the core [basic] curriculum and performance standards in order to make choices," predicts National PTA spokesperson Arnold Fege.

Risks and reforms

The challenges facing America's schools are complex and difficult to solve. Still, the national mood is optimistic. Excellent teachers, willing businesspeople, enthusiastic parents, and talented students are already involved in the quest for

improvement. With the support of government, school administration, and education experts, they can go far toward creating schools of which everyone can be proud.

As Patricia Albjerg Graham, former dean of Harvard University's Graduate School of Education says:

> The schools will not flourish, and our children will not be educated, unless the entire nation recognizes and acts to improve the schools. . . . The crisis is upon all of us. We—family, government, higher education, and business—must sustain our schools. Unless we do so, our prospects are dim: our nation is weakened, our democracy diminished, and our future limited.

The future of America's students does not depend solely on the creativity of teachers. It also lies in the hands of government officials, school administrators, and above all, involved parents.

Organizations to Contact

The following organizations provide information about teaching, school curricula, parent involvement in education, alternative schooling, and other education-related subjects.

American Federation of Teachers (AFT)
555 New Jersey Avenue NW
Washington, DC 20001
(202) 879-4400

The AFT is one of the largest organizations of teachers and other educational employees in the United States. Its objectives include promoting professionalism in teaching, improving working conditions, wages, and job security for members, and ensuring equal-education opportunities for all Americans. AFT publishes a quarterly magazine, *American Educator*.

Coalition of Essential Schools
c/o Dr. Theodore R. Sizer, Chairman
Brown University
P.O. Box 1969
Providence, RI 02912
(401) 863-2045

Founded in 1984, the coalition works to reform secondary school curricula and improve student learning through simplifying school structure and adjusting school priorities. It publishes a bimonthly newsletter, *Horace*.

The Metropolitan Life Survey of the American Teacher
P.O. Box 807
Madison Square Station
New York, NY 10159-0807

The survey is published annually and contains teachers' views on current issues in education. Topics include relationships between teachers and students, developments in the teaching profession, links between parents and teachers, and concerns over violence in public schools.

National Congress of Parents and Teachers (National PTA)
700 North Rush Street
Chicago, IL 60611
(312) 670-6782

The PTA is a volunteer organization that unites the forces of the home, school, and community to promote the welfare of children. Its projects have dealt with the effects of television on young people, the prevention of alcohol and drug abuse, and parent education. The National PTA issues monthly and annual publications, as well as informational pamphlets for use by local PTAs.

National Center on Education and the Economy
39 State Street, Suite 500
Rochester, NY 14614
(716) 546-7620

The center works to draw public attention to the link between economic growth and the skills and abilities of the people who contribute to that growth. It provides advice and assistance to educational, training, and retraining programs. It sponsors the National Alliance for Restructuring Education program and the New Standards Project.

National Committee for Citizens in Education (NCCE)
900 Second Street NE, Suite 8
Washington, DC 20002
(202) 462-7688

NCCE works to improve the quality of public schools by encouraging parents and the general public to become more involved in education. The committee publishes *Network*, an information periodical, six times a year. It also publishes handbooks, brochures, and pamphlets on educational issues of interest to parent and citizen groups.

National Education Association (NEA)
1201 16th Street NW
Washington, DC 20036
(202) 833-4000

The NEA is the largest professional education organization in the world. Its goals include improving public education and classroom conditions, as well as increasing the salaries and benefits of school employees. The NEA publishes books, filmstrips, and informational leaflets, as well as its magazine, *NEA Today*, which is issued eight times a year.

National Homeschool Association (NHA)
P.O. Box 290
Hartland, MI 48353-0290
(313) 632-5208

The association promotes public awareness of home education. It encourages communication and the exchange of experiences among home-schooling families. NHA publishes a quarterly newsletter, *Circle of Correspondence*.

Suggestions for Further Reading

Michael D. Biskup and Charles P. Cozic, eds., *Youth Violence*. San Diego: Greenhaven Press, 1992.

Charles P. Cozic, ed., *Education in America*. San Diego: Greenhaven Press, 1992.

Tracy Kidder, *Among Schoolchildren*. Boston: Houghton Mifflin, 1989.

Sherri McCarthy-Tucker, *Coping with Special Needs Classmates*. New York: Rosen Publishing Group, 1993.

Works Consulted

Sam Allis, "Laying Siege to Seniority," *Time*, December 23, 1991.

———, "Testing, Testing, Testing," *Time*, July 15, 1991.

———, "Whose America?" *Time*, July 8, 1991.

———, "Why 180 Days Aren't Enough," *Time*, September 2, 1991.

James M. Banner Jr., "The Parallel School," *Phi Delta Kappan*, February 1992.

David Beers, "True Revolution," *Mother Jones*, November/December 1992.

Philip Bigler and Karen Lockard, *Failing Grades: A Teacher's Report Card on Education in America*. Arlington, VA: Vandamere Press, 1992.

"Blues in School," *Today Show*, NBC, May 12, 1994.

Gerald W. Bracey, "No Magic Bullet," *Phi Delta Kappan*, February 1993.

———, "The Third Bracey Report on the Condition of Public Education," *Phi Delta Kappan*, October 1993.

Diane Brady, "The World Learns," *Mother Jones*, September/October 1993.

B. David Brooks and Mark E. Kann, "The Schools' Role in Weaving Values Back into the Fabric of Society," *The Education Digest*, April 1993.

The Budget of the United States Government for the Fiscal Year 1993. Washington, DC: U.S. Government Printing Office, 1992.

Dale D. Buss, "Parents Edgy over Classroom Groupthink," *Christianity Today*, September 13, 1993.

Erik Calonius, "The Big Payoff from Lotteries," *Fortune*, March 25, 1991.

Charles S. Clark, "Education Standards," *CQ Researcher*, March 11, 1994.

Josh Clark, "Pro-Choice," *Mother Jones*, September/October 1993.

Michele Collison, "Saying No to School Choice," *Black Enterprise*, July 1991.

Linda Darling-Hammond, "Achieving Our Goals: Superficial or Structural Reforms?" *Phi Delta Kappan*, December 1990.

Diane Dismuke, "Helping Community, Helping Themselves," *NEA Today*, September 1993.

————, "Private Sector Eyes Public Schools," *NEA Today*, November 1992.

M. P. Dunleavey, "Reforming the 3 R's: Blueprints for the Schools of Tomorrow," *Publishers Weekly*, February 21, 1994.

The Economist, "Teacher in Disgrace," March 6, 1993.

Stanley M. Elam et al., "The 25th Annual Phi Delta Kappa/Gallup Poll of the Public's Attitudes Toward the Public Schools," *Phi Delta Kappan*, October 1993.

Electronic Learning, "School Choice: Will It Save or 'Gut' Schools?" March 1993.

David Ellis, "Knowledge for Sale," *Time*, June 8, 1992.

Kevin Fedarko, "Can I Copy Your Homework—And Represent You in Court?" *Time*, September 21, 1992.

Joseph A. Fernandez and John Underwood, *Tales Out of School*. Boston: Little, Brown, 1993.

Douglas Frantz and Elizabeth Shogren, "Conservative Fire Spreads with School Board Sparks," *Los Angeles Times*, December 11, 1993.

Anthony Giardina, "Fighting in the Schoolyard," *Harper's Magazine*, April 1994.

Nancy Gibbs, "Schools for Profit," *Time*, October 17, 1994.

———, "Starving the Schools," *Time*, April 15, 1991.

Larry Gordon, "Few Gains Seen in Nation's Schools," *Los Angeles Times*, April 9, 1993.

Patricia Albjerg Graham, *SOS: Sustain Our Schools*. New York: Hill and Wang, 1992.

Beatrice Gross and Ronald Gross, eds., *The Great School Debate*. New York: Simon and Schuster, 1985.

Ted Gup, "What Makes This School Work?" *Time*, December 21, 1992.

Donna Harrington-Lueker, "Toward a New National Yardstick," *The American School Board Journal*, February 1994.

Dennis Hevesi, "Cortines Moves to Devise New Multicultural Curriculum," *The New York Times*, November 18, 1993.

Robert M. Huelskamp, "The Second Coming of the Sandia Report," *The Education Digest*, September 1993.

Jet, "EEOC Rules That Texas' Teacher Test Is Biased," October 3, 1988.

Susan Moore Johnson, *Teachers at Work*. New York: Basic Books, 1990.

Kenneth Jost, "Private Management of Public Schools," *CQ Researcher*, March 25, 1994.

Barbara Kantrowitz, "Is It Summer Already?" *Newsweek*, March 22, 1993.

———, "Take the Money and Run," *Newsweek*, October 11, 1993.

Jeanne Kiefner and Janet Hughes, "Should Public Schools Distribute Condoms?" *NEA Today*, October 1993.

Richard Kigel, *The Frontier Years of Abe Lincoln*. New York: Walker and Co., 1986.

Jonathan Kozol, *Savage Inequalities*. New York: Crown Publishers, 1991.

Richard Lacayo, "School's Out—of Cash," *Time*, April 5, 1993.

Jeff Leeds, "Study Finds Johnny Can't Write Too Well," *Los Angeles Times*, June 8, 1994.

Michael D. Lemonick, "Tomorrow's Lesson: Learn or Perish," *Time* (Special Issue), Fall 1992.

Howard Libit, "Negative Report Issued on State's Math Students," *Los Angeles Times*, April 9, 1993.

Nancy Linnon et al., "Schools That Work," *U.S. News & World Report*, May 27, 1991.

Robert Emmet Long, ed., *American Education*. New York: H. W. Wilson Press, 1984.

Victoria Lytle, "Memphis in Motion," *NEA Today*, May/June 1991.

———, "Reform Boosts Pay but Pace Slows," *NEA Today*, April 1993.

Kimberly J. McLarin, "School Panel Approves Fiscal Equity Plan," *The New York Times*, April 14, 1994.

Jean Merl, "Are Private Schools Better?" *Los Angeles Times*, March 29, 1992.

———, "Quest for the Right School Can Be Complex Odyssey," *Los Angeles Times*, March 30, 1992.

———, "Rethinking the Move Away from Single-Sex Schools," *Los Angeles Times*, April 1, 1992.

Michael Meyer, "Another Lost Generation," *Newsweek*, May 4, 1992.

Emily Mitchell, "Do the Poor Deserve Bad Schools?" *Time*, October 14, 1991.

Charles E. Moore, "Twelve Secrets of Restructured Schools," *The Education Digest*, December 1993.

Tom Morganthau et al., "It's Not Just New York …" *Newsweek*, March 9, 1992.

Lance Morrow, "Childhood's End," *Time*, March 9, 1992.

Sara Mosley, "Dim Bulb," *The New Republic*, January 18, 1993.

Donna E. Muncey and Patrick J. McQuillan, "Preliminary Findings from a Five-Year Study of the Coalition of Essential Schools," *Phi Delta Kappan*, February 1993.

Joseph Murphy, *Restructuring Schools*. New York: Teachers College Press, 1991.

A Nation Prepared: Teachers for the Twenty-First Century. New York: Carnegie Forum on Education and the Economy, 1986.

NEA Today, "Teacher Pay Up 3.6% in Past Year," September 1993.

Nancy R. Needham, "The Fad That Faded," *NEA Today*, May 1987.

The New York Times, "Voters in California Reject Proposal on School Vouchers," November 3, 1993.

Rod Nordland, "Deadly Lessons," *Newsweek*, March 9, 1992.

Linda Olasov and Jane Petrillo, "Meeting Health Needs Through Kentucky's New Family Resource Centers and Youth Services Centers," *Journal of School Health*, February 1994.

Richard N. Ostling, "A Revolution Hoping for a Miracle," *Time*, April 29, 1991.

Helen Pate-Bain et al., "Class Size Does Make a Difference," *Phi Delta Kappan*, November 1992.

Neal R. Peirce, "Public Charter Schools: Why Not?" *Nation's Cities Weekly*, June 10, 1991.

David Perkins, *Smart Schools: From Training Memories to Educating Minds*. New York: The Free Press, 1992.

Susan Phillips, "Racial Tensions in Schools," *CQ Researcher*, January 7, 1994.

Chris Pipho, "Bipartisan Charter Schools," *Phi Delta Kappan*, October 1993.

Leah Pisano, "Edutrain: A Charter School for At-Risk Kids," *The Education Digest*, January 1994.

Arlynn L. Presser, "Revolution Needed," *National Review*, October 7, 1991.

David E. Purpel, "Moral Education: An Idea Whose Time Has Gone," *The Clearing House*, May/June 1991.

Ruth E. Randall, "Private-Practice Teachers and Charter Schools," *The Education Digest*, April 1993.

John Martin Rich, "The Conflict in Moral Education: Teaching Principles or Virtues," *The Clearing House*, May/June 1991.

Richard W. Riley, "The Secretary of Education on Reinventing Education," *The Education Digest*, January 1994.

Jonathan Schorr, "California's Experiment on Your Schools," *The New York Times*, October 30, 1993.

The Seattle Times, "It Was One Gang Against Another," March 25, 1994.

Daniel Seymour and Terry Seymour, *America's Best Classrooms*. Princeton, NJ: Peterson's Guides, 1992.

Walter Shapiro, "Tough Choice," *Time*, September 16, 1991.

Ken Sidey, "Book Series Leaves the Wrong 'Impressions,'" *Christianity Today*, January 14, 1991.

Betty Jo Simmons, "Classroom at Home," *The American School Board Journal*, February 1994.

Robert J. Simpson, "Education 2000 AD: A Peek into the Future," *USA Today*, January 1992.

Jill Smolowe, "Crusade for the Classroom," *Time*, November 1, 1993.

Jackie E. Swensson, "New NCTE Policy on Class Size and Teacher Workload," *English Journal*, February 1991.

Abigail Thernstrom, "Hobson's Choice," *The New Republic*, July 15 and 22, 1991.

Susan Tifft, "Better Safe Than Sorry?" *Time*, January 21, 1991.

Thomas Toch, "The Exodus," *U.S. News & World Report*, December 9, 1991.

James Traub, "Can Separate Be Equal?" *Harper's Magazine*, June 1994.

David Van Biema, "The Great Tax Switch," *Time*, March 28, 1994.

Ernest van den Haag, "Why Do American Kids Learn So Little?" *National Review*, August 3, 1992.

The Wall Street Journal, "The Charter Half-Step," February 23, 1994.

Jonathan Weber, "'Schools Within Schools' Pay Off in Philadelphia," *Los Angeles Times*, June 12, 1994.

Isabel Wilkerson, "Chicago Learns How Hard It Is to Better Schools," *The New York Times*, October 20, 1993.

Arthur E. Wise and Jane Leibbrand, "Accreditation and the Creation of a Profession of Teaching," *Phi Delta Kappan*, October 1993.

George H. Wood, *Schools That Work*. New York: Penguin Books, 1992.

Richard L Worsnop, "Gambling Boom," *CQ Researcher*, March 18, 1994.

Index

About the Author

Diane Yancey began writing for her own entertainment when she was thirteen, while living in Grass Valley, California. Later she graduated from Augustana College in Illinois. She now pursues a writing career in the Pacific Northwest, where she lives with her husband, two daughters, and two cats. Her interests include collecting old books, building miniature houses, and traveling.

Ms. Yancey's books include *Desperadoes and Dynamite*, *The Reunification of Germany*, *The Hunt for Hidden Killers*, and a book on the U.S. Camel Corps.

Picture Credits